How I Came to Berlin

How I Came to Berlin

An Artist's Journey from Belfast and the London Blitz to a Cold-War City

Elizabeth Shaw

Foreword by Anne Schneider
Edited with an Afterword by
Sabine Egger & Fergal Lenehan

THE LILLIPUT PRESS
DUBLIN

First published in English 2025 by
THE LILLIPUT PRESS

62–63 Sitric Road,
Arbour Hill,
Dublin 7,
Ireland
www.lilliputpress.ie

10 9 8 7 6 5 4 3 2 1

A CIP record for this title is available from The British Library.

Paperback ISBN 978 1 84351 952 2
eBook ISBN 978 1 84351 953 9

Set in 12 pt on 16.5 pt Adobe Jenson Pro and Adobe Caslon Pro by Compuscript
Cover design by Katie Tooke, katie-tooke.com
Printed and bound in Czechia by Finidr

CONTENTS

FOREWORD

My parents are still very close to me and, as always, you only realize what has been left unsaid when they are no longer around. Some of the things they did I only understand now, some I still cannot comprehend. But I think that's normal: parents live their own lives and children shouldn't try to judge them in retrospect.

When our mother died in 1992, we, my brother Patrick and I, found in her will the wish that her ashes would be scattered in the Irish Sea so that they would reach the Atlantic Ocean when the wind was favourable. Everyone in the family agreed, but making it happen was quite complicated, at least as far as the ashes were concerned. The really nice thing about this, despite the sadness of the occasion, was that we went to Ireland for the first time and met an incredible number of relatives there who organized everything and finally found a place, Carlingford in County Louth, on whose pier we scattered the ashes into the Irish Sea. It was wonderful to hear the family stories. We were both over forty years old and had never seen the country from which our mother had come to Germany. We only really knew the stories about her relatives from England; her siblings had all stayed there and had families there. We saw them very rarely after the Wall was built in 1961; only a few ventured into East Berlin. The long period without direct contact with relatives in Ireland, England and Wales naturally had an impact on the intensity of the relationships, but I know for sure that if we decide to visit them, we will be warmly welcomed.

Until his death in 2006, my brother Patrick worked very intensively on our parents' estate, maintaining contacts with publishers and organizing exhibitions. Now that I'm looking after the drawings and the books, I realize that I know very little about my mother's life before 1946. There are drawings by her for the English monthly magazine *Lilliput*, illustrations, political caricatures and sketches. I tracked down a supplier in London on the Internet who still has old posters drawn by her in stock.

When they came to Berlin, our parents were twenty-six and thirty-eight years old respectively. They hadn't yet made up their minds artistically, they were curious and willing to become involved in something new. That was certainly difficult and also beautiful, as it is with artists, an up and down that fosters creativity. For Patrick and me, the hallmarks of such an eventful artistic life were always a normal part of our childhood – listening to foreign languages, discussions late into the night, books everywhere, going to the cinema and theatre together, hiking and swimming, the Baltic Sea, stories about the family and, of course, drawing and painting.

To this day, I am always delighted by the watercolours and pencil and pen drawings by my mother that I find in the many sketch books and in the drawing cabinet. There are drawings of the apartment in Berlin's Treskowstraße that complement the memories in my head. Drawing was obviously my mother's way of intensively engaging with her surroundings. There are some books in German in which this can still be admired: *Spiegelbilder* [Mirror Images], *Das dicke Elizabeth-Shaw-Buch* [The Big Elizabeth Shaw Book] and *Eine Feder am Meeresstrand* [A Feather on the Seashore].

Better-known than these titles aimed at an adult audience are, of course, my mother's children's books. These still remain very present today: Kinderbuchverlag Berlin, the first port of call for beautifully designed books for a young audience in the former German Democratic Republic, is now part of the Beltz Publishing Group, and my mother's books are available and still popular more than thirty years since the fall of the Berlin Wall. It was more than sixty years ago in 1963 that *Der kleine Angsthase* [The Timid Rabbit] was first published, and it is my experience that people of all ages remember this book as part of their childhood or of their reading time with their own children.

Exhibitions of Elizabeth Shaw's work have been held in all of the eastern German states. In 2010 we were lucky enough to be able to show the original drawings of some of her children's books at Burg Wissem in Troisdorf near Cologne, a unique museum specializing in artistic picture-book illustration. It is perhaps also worth mentioning that there has been a primary school called after Elizabeth Shaw – the Elizabeth-Shaw-Grundschule – in Berlin-Pankow for many years. In addition, there are always small theatre groups that produce very original performances based on the stories from her children's books.

In 2023 we gave the original drawings from the children's books to the Staatsbibliothek zu Berlin [The State Library of Berlin], and in 2024 the original drawings of the illustrated books for adults were given to the *Deutsches Buch- und Schriftmuseum* [German Museum of Books and Writing] at the German National Library in Leipzig.

All in all, it can be said that my mother's work is anything but forgotten today in Germany. But what about *How I Came to Berlin?* The autobiography, first published by the Aufbau Verlag in 1990, has always appealed to me. Many people in Germany know Elizabeth Shaw's children's books but know hardly anything about her life. The problems of integration, arriving and living in a country that is completely different, whose people have had completely different experiences – all of this is very much a part of normality today. I often think about the concept of home – or *Heimat* in German – which I cannot really define for myself. Perhaps everything written in the memoir is this sense of home for me, the totality of my ancestors' experiences. For this edition I had to scan the English-language text written on a typewriter and transferred it to the computer. I had to read everything very carefully, including the description of a 'walk' through London in 1940. How horrible that must have been, at night, without any light, without a soul on the street! My mother and her siblings had the experience of being recognized as foreigners by their accent and their choice of clothing when the family moved from Ireland to England. You have to cope with all of that and, if possible, turn it into a type of positive energy. My mum went to London on her own as soon as she finished school and started her career as an artist, perhaps helped by the experiences she had already had. I only realized some things when I read her memoir. I found images I remembered and also find myself in this text, for example in Lyme Regis, a southern English harbour town, where I was on holiday in 2008: only when I reread the book did I fully realize that my parents were already there, with me, in 1948.

I think my mother was happy with her life. She was successful in her work, had her family in Germany, lots of friends, and she was inquisitive and curious. She was able to contribute to society with her very own talents. My knowledge of my mother is expanding, and it is a pleasure to meet her again and again.

Anne Schneider

2025

I

I

I and Pangur Bán, my cat,
'Tis a like task we are at;
Hunting mice is his delight,
Hunting words I sit all night.

'Gainst the wall he sets his eye
Full and fierce and sharp and sly;
'Gainst the wall of knowledge I
All my little wisdom try.

Translated from the Irish by Kuno Meyer
Author unknown, ninth century

The first question I have been frequently asked since I came to live in Germany is whether I am related to George Bernard Shaw. To answer this, I can only quote the famous G.B.S. himself, who did a little research on the subject of his forefathers. He wrote: 'I have no trace in me of the commercially imported North Spanish strain which passes for aboriginal Irish: I am a typical Irishman of the Danish, Norman, Cromwellian, and (of course) Scotch invasions.'

This could apply to me too, except that G.B.S. belonged to the eastern Dublin Shaws, and I belong to the western Sligo Shaws, where some of that North Spanish strain was added by my grandmother McKim.

As you see the Irish are very conscious of clan and history.

The second question which I have been frequently asked since I came here is why did I come to Berlin. To answer this, I have to think a long way back.

I was born in a Protestant bed, delivered by a Catholic doctor. This was in 1920, in the middle of Belfast, when the 'Troubles', the sectarian violence, once again escalated in the city. It was advisable then to keep away from the windows because of stones aimed at them, or because of rifle shots from neighbouring rooftops. It was dangerous for a Catholic to be seen entering a Protestant house. We had a maid called Bridget, of whom I was very fond. She was a Catholic and one day a note was dropped through the letterbox saying that if we did not send her away, she would not be the only one to suffer. Such threats were to be taken seriously, and so one of my earliest memories is of sitting on my mother's arm at the street door and being told to wave goodbye to Bridget, as she walked away with her suitcase. I realize now that this public farewell was staged for the benefit of unseen hostile observers.

We lived above the York Street branch of the Ulster Bank on the corner of Earl Street. The rooms were large and dusty with high, dirty windows, barred at the back of the house, some with stained glass, decorated in the style of the turn of the century. Opposite us towered the massive red-brick Gallaher's Tobacco factory. Life was regulated by 'Gallaher's Horn', the factory siren, which sounded in the morning, at midday and in the late afternoon. The air was pervaded with the odour of raw tobacco, stale beer and dust. Horse-drawn carts rattled from the docks to the station, and tall trams whined and clanged as they swayed past. Unease and poverty.

My father made hasty exits and entrances to and from the bank office on the ground floor. He swallowed his meals rapidly, retailing the events of the day, often stammering a little. Banks were not then so anonymous as they are today, and his attitude to the customers was paternalistic. 'Old so-and-so was in today,' I remember him saying, 'and he wanted some money, but I told him he couldn't have it, for he'd only spend it on drink!'

My father was always anxious to be finished with the office work so that he could do something which interested him. He was a self-educated man. No one could follow his method in arithmetical calculation, but the answer was always right. He had a wide range of interests and activities, but never in his life did he learn to boil an egg or darn a sock, for he was a man of the nineteenth century and such matters were taken care of by his mother, then his sister and then his wife. He had a daily programme with which he let nothing interfere. It began with dumbbell exercises, then off to the office to earn a living, then sport in the fresh air, before he settled down to read his many books. His native interest in the past had been sublimated into an interest in history generally and he pursued this with the detachment of a dedicated librarian. This fondness for reading influenced me at an early age and I still find the smell of a newly unfolded newspaper as enticing as the odour of fresh rolls is to some. Before breakfast my father put on his hat, took his walking stick and walked rapidly as usual to the small newspaper shop in York Street. He snatched a little fresh air and picked up his copy of the daily *Northern Whig*, as well as the weekly *Punch* and *Illustrated London News*, when they were due. There was no television and no radio in those days, and one read the papers to find out what was happening – according to the viewpoint of the paper, of course. I remember a drawing in the *London News* which depicted a monster rather like Jabberwocky in *Alice in Wonderland*, entitled *A Bolshevik*, and well calculated to raise a shudder.

There were no restrictions as to what we read in the extensive collection of my father's books, which began with a faded pink paperback series of the *Penny Poets* and continued with the bestsellers of his youth, Maurice Jokai, Marie Bashkirtseff, an early paperback of Tolstoy and fat volumes of history, all signed, with the date of purchase, in spidery handwriting.

When the papers and magazines had been read, they were stacked in a small dark cupboard room, known as the Paper Pantry. There we used to rummage among old tracts of the abstinence movement – Grandfather Shaw had drunk too much – and shuddered at woodcuts depicting the fate of little girls driven bleeding out into the snow by an inebriated father. Our parents' love letters were there, tied in bundles, and there were newspaper cuttings of my father's shy attempts to take a course in writing fiction, offered by the *Irish Times*, and the rude reply to 'G. Wash' saying that he had no talent and might as well give up at once. In the Paper Pantry there were many secrets of which we never spoke, and our parents did not either, but they induced a kind of gentle understanding. We browsed too through stacks of illustrated magazines dating back to the 1890s. Reading about politics and history was very much a part of daily life in our high house, overlooking the shabby rooftops of dockland Belfast.

2

Because we lived in the midst of a dirty and dusty city and because we might have inherited a Shaw weakness of the lungs from which several relatives had died, we spent all our holidays in the country. Mostly we went to our maternal grandparents in the Magowan farmhouse among the bumpy green hills of County Armagh, the blue tip of Slieve Gullion in the Mourne Mountains always visible in the distance. The Magowan house on the outskirts of the village Mountnorris was built in neat eighteenth-century style. Behind the house was an older one, used for storage, and connected to the later building by the stone-flagged kitchen, which was the centre of the house. Once there had been an opening in the roof to let out smoke. From the kitchen a room had been built on, a small dining room, which opened on to the yard, with its stables, dairy and various outhouses. A house permeated with a long changing past and a paradoxical stability.

The Magowans had come over from Scotland and settled in Mountnorris some three centuries before. They came, it is said, looking for work, and became servitors of the O'Hanlon clan, to whom the land then belonged. Later they were joined by Presbyterian settlers from the lowlands of Scotland and French Huguenot refugees. They formed a close-knit community with much intermarriage. Many Scottish traditions were preserved, including an emphasis on the importance of education and a fierce independence. Nonconformism was particularly manifest among the Irvines, my grandmother's family – her eldest brother being perhaps an exception, as he became a professor of theology at Magee University. A second brother became a doctor, practised abroad, then returned to his native village. He wrote books about medicine and social progress, in which he quoted extensively George Bernard Shaw, condemning the trade in patent medicines. He preached tolerance in religion as well and put his principles into practice by marrying a Catholic midwife from Cork.

We used to watch our great-aunt Mary, dressed in ancient silk dresses and a toque styled around 1880, walking down the hill to the Catholic chapel to attend Mass on Sunday, while Granny in her best black hat set out in the opposite direction to the Presbyterian Meeting House. We did not join her because we belonged to the Church of Ireland, Protestant too, but the congregation knelt to pray and sang hymns almost Popish, said Granny. Uncle Gilbert, the doctor, did not go to any church, but smoked a big cigar at home, which yellowed his white moustache, and tilted his straw hat over a sardonic eye as he viewed the scene.

Uncle Gilbert's eccentricities were accepted by his understanding siblings, for they had been brought up in a harsh Calvinist tradition: family were not allowed to learn a profession, they were all expected to marry and raise families. My granny, the eldest, transferred her frustrated ambition to her children. They should all study, get scholarships, get on in life – the girls too!

Elizabeth Shaw's grandmother, Sarah Ann Magowan, circa 1936.

The Irvines were small and wiry, energetic and tough. The Magowans were emotional and often darkly depressive. Those of her nine children who took after the Magowans had a rough time with Granny. However, aided by the village schoolmaster, Mr Morrison, most of them went her way. The eldest was her special pride, as he became a diplomat and was even knighted. The two eldest girls won scholarships to Trinity College in Dublin, and the younger boys went in for medicine and veterinary surgery.

Trinity College Dublin, 1916. Front row, first from left: Elizabeth's mother Mary Magowan, third from left: her sister and godmother of Elizabeth, Jane Elizabeth Magowan.

Our grandfather, whom we called Papa, like our very young uncles and aunts did, used to pick us up with horse and trap at Goraghwood Station,[1] which we reached by train from Belfast. The train had no corridor in those days, and the compartments were locked and unlocked at each station. We all climbed into the swaying trap, and it was great to be allowed to sit in front with Papa and hold the reins. During the day Papa was mostly outside, working on the farm. In the evening he would come into the kitchen with the horse collars and harness and hang them on the wall. Then the wicks of the oil lamps were trimmed and lit, first burning with a low flame, then turned up high to a soft glow. A time came when Papa was ill and there he was, sitting up in bed in a white nightshirt, smiling kindly when we came to visit, but we knew it was a sickbed visit, and I was frightened.

Then he died, and I thought I heard his ghost walking in the attic. In front of the house was an enormous, very old beech tree. Its rustling leaves were the music of the night, and one of the girls who worked in the house told me that once when she returned in the evening, she saw a banshee in the tree, looking down at her. One day I went out of the house and there was an old man with a white beard sitting on the milk churn standing under the beech tree smiling kindly. I thought for a moment it was Papa's ghost and nearly fainted.

'Don't bring white hawthorn into the house, it brings bad luck!' 'Never open an umbrella in the house!' for the same reason, and if you should be unlucky enough to spill some salt, a pinch thrown over the left shoulder with the right hand will undo the evil spell.

There was quite a social life in the stone-flagged kitchen. Granny was the central figure, dressed in black, small, brisk and sharp, churning butter in the big wooden hand churn, out to feed the hens, 'Birdie, birdie, birdie!' – cooking porridge and chicken soup, calling the men on the farm to dinner on the washed wooden kitchen table. Meals consisted of potatoes, home-made bread, salty butter, bacon, porridge, eggs, oatcakes, beans, cabbage and chicken. All produce of the farm, except tea and sugar, which were bought at Joe Hare the grocer down the bog road.

We had a glimpse of living history here, of a lifestyle which had hardly changed in three hundred years or more. Later when the boys were earning well, electricity was installed in the house, running water replaced the pump in the yard, and a bathroom and toilet were built. A little Austin minicar replaced the horse and trap, and young uncle Irvine, the veterinary surgeon, introduced fancy experiments in the byre – the cowshed – installing water taps with levers, which the cows could push with their noses themselves and drink when thirsty.

Down the hill, towards the Chapel Road, sometimes we met in winter poor children carrying big bundles of firewood on their backs, which they had gathered from the hedges. They had bare blue feet and running noses.

'It's a brave day!' they greeted politely.

'Brave day!' we replied.

In the country poverty was painful too.

In spite of the success of her children in their various careers, and the opportunities they offered her to visit them in far-flung places, Granny never went more than fifty miles from the village in her long life – because of the hens, she said. She rose every day at six and cooked her oatmeal porridge. When the lamps were lit in the evening, she did the crossword puzzle in the newspaper, with the help of all present in the kitchen, or read a book before going to bed at nine. Sometimes we slept in another bed in her room, and then I watched with half-shut eyes as she undid her knot of hair and a long grey pigtail fell down her back. Then she took off her dress and her knee-length frilled cotton knickers, put on a long white nightdress and got into bed, blowing out the candle by her bedside.

3

Granny killed chickens by wringing their necks. At the other farmhouse in Belcoo,[1] in the west of Ireland, where we often stayed, our cousin Maud chopped their heads off with an axe. Maud and Kathleen Tate were relations on our father's side of the family, and life was quite different there to life at Granny's in Mountnorris.

The Tate sisters were cousins of ours. When their mother died Kathleen was adopted by our Shaw grandmother, who lived with my father in Belfast until her death in 1912. Maud kept house for her father, Dr Tate, in Belcoo, and when my father married, Kathleen came to live with her. Maud was tall and red-haired, big teeth, jolly laugh. She ran the farm. Kathleen, frail, slight and pale, drifted about, cooking little scones and turning out meals at unexpected intervals, giggling quite a lot in a friendly way. Both were unmarried. It was leisurely in Belcoo. Time did not seem to matter. No Magowan ambitions were pursued. I cannot remember seeing books in the house, but there was a small glass veranda above the front door where a pile of old magazines lay among pots of geraniums, where we liked to sit in the warm sunshine, reading and enjoying the strange odour of the plants. Maud and Kathleen must have gone to school somewhere, but they never mentioned it. The spirit of Mr Morrison, the village schoolmaster in Mountnorris, was far away. There was a piano in the living room, and an oil painting by Jack Yeats, brother of the poet William Butler Yeats, hung on the wall. They were neighbours.

'But whatever happened to poor Willie?' mused Maud.

People dropped past – a curate who played the piano and sang, armed customs guards from the frontier down the road, and there was much talk and laughter. The sisters lived in a house called Danesfort, among fine wild scenery of mountains and lakes. Sometimes we went fishing on the lake with Maud. A stream ran along the bottom of the garden, where trout swam in small deep pools and coloured dragonflies darted over the water. There was a short drive up to the house, lined with fir trees and a stretch of meadow at the side. On this there was a hillock with a few trees on top, and inside these was a ring of stones, the grave of some old Danes, who had invaded the coast here around the ninth century and given the house its name. The grave had been examined by archaeologists but then left undisturbed, because otherwise, it was said, it would bring bad luck.

A little along the road was the quiet lake, Upper Loch Macnean, on the left, and moorland on the right. At the crossroads there was a small pool known as the Wishing Well, a circle of moss-covered stones surrounding a spring of delicious clear water, from which we used to drink with hollowed hands, and then walk round the well and make a wish, which should come true.

Opposite Danesfort lived old Mrs Doherty, in a tiny, white-washed cottage with a thatched roof. When Kathleen had baked some fresh scones, we were told to take a few over to Mrs Doherty. She was very poor. Hens wandered in and out of the cottage, roosting on the beams, and when we asked if we could scatter some grain for them, Mrs. Doherty said yes, but then 'Not too much!' Once she showed us a present she had received, a lump of fat bacon, wrapped carefully in a cloth, like a precious stone. We travelled from Belfast to Belcoo by train. In Enniskillen we changed to a small old-fashioned train, which we sarcastically called 'The Belcoo Express'. The train took off when it suited the railway staff, rather like Kathleen's cooking habits. When it was time for us to return to Belfast, Maud waited until she heard the engine whistle, and then she went down to the field to catch the pony, which was to transport our luggage to the station.

Today this all sounds very idyllic. For us from the city, with its social tensions, with its dirt and noise, it was indeed.

Was it really such an intact world?

I would say, yes.

The frightful poverty, the damp climate, which encouraged tubercular disease, drove people away, but the water was pure, the air unpolluted, there were no old plastic bags on the shore of the lake, and scarcely a car on the rough roads.

4

Most summers we visited our Aunt Annie. She was my father's sister. As she was a widow, she lived for a time with him in Belfast, and when he married, he bought her a house on the north coast, in the seaside resort of Portstewart, so that she could support herself and her daughter by running a boarding house for holidaymakers. We did not like staying there because the house smelt of cabbage and burnt cake, the unsuccessful result of Cousin Peggy's cookery course. We did not like Aunt Annie or her daughter, who complained continuously, and as soon as we could we set off on expeditions with sandwiches and bathing suits. We walked along the promenade, past the small harbour. When the tide was in, each wave threw up a jet of water through a hole in the rocks. We followed a cliff path, crossed a small shell-strewn beach and came at last to the wide, white strand, washed by the strong waves of the Atlantic. In the background rose high sand hills and, in the distance, one could see the blue mountains of Donegal. Sometimes in the evening we went out over the stretch of grass and sea-pinks at the back of the house to the rocks beyond, clear pools between them when the tide was out, where velvety sea anemones waved, and tiny sea creatures darted to and fro. There too we could watch dramatic scarlet sunsets over the western water.

How lucky we were to have relatives so well-placed and willing to receive a family with four children!

The Shaw family in Portstewart, 1933. From left to right: Elizabeth, sister Matilda, mother Mary Shaw, father George W. Shaw, brothers Patrick and Warren (in front).

5

The Shaws probably came over to Ireland in the seventeenth century, as adventurers, as Cromwellian soldiers, in the English army of occupation. They received grants of land as a reward for their services. They belonged to what was known as the Protestant Ascendancy, the dominant influence in social life. They considered themselves a cut above the Magowans, who were tenant farmers. The Shaws and their kin raised horses which lost races, went salmon fishing and drank the good whiskey. When money was short, they managed to get another grant of land, as long as that was possible, or emigrated to the colonies.

Elizabeth's grandfather George William Shaw, circa 1902.

Grandfather Shaw died in 1888, leaving debts and a widow with six children, the eldest being my eighteen-year-old father. After a vain attempt to run the estate most of it was sold, and he took a job as a clerk in the Ulster Bank in Ballina. He worked hard for a small wage, sent most of it home to his mother and cured himself of threatened tuberculosis by taking long walks over the mountains. Finally, he was appointed manager of the Ulster Bank in York Street, Belfast. There were spacious, rent-free living quarters over the bank, and he moved in with his mother, his widowed sister and her daughter and Kathleen Tate. So the female members of the family were taken care of. The younger brothers dispersed, emigrated to New Zealand, or died of tuberculosis. One settled in Dublin and founded a family of staunch republicans down there. My mother, then Mary Magowan, studied languages at Trinity College in Dublin, and during vacations she used to work as assistant teacher in her old boarding school in Whitehead, not far from Belfast. The headmistress of the school, Miss McKeowan, had an eye on my father as an eligible bachelor and a good match for one of her girls, and she used to send them as messengers to consult him on bank business. With Mary she had success at last. My mother broke off her studies at Trinity College, much to the chagrin of teachers and feminist friends, for she was doing well. But the difference in age was great – almost thirty years – and she felt that she should not wait. They married in 1918, and the widowed sister and Kathleen Tate were hustled out to make way for the bride.

River estuary in Ballina, Ireland, 1982.[1]

6

Once when my little brother was about six, he was riding his tricycle along the street in front of our house in Belfast when he was accosted by a bigger boy, who blocked his path and demanded belligerently: 'What sort of man are you?' My little brother hesitated. He knew that the wrong answer could cost him a bloody nose. 'I'm a Christian!' he said, at last. 'Then get away from a good Protestant like me!' growled the big boy, taken aback. My little brother pedalled away hastily to the fortress of our house, the Ulster Bank.

As banks are, it was solidly built of red brick and stucco, with a marble base. Iron gates closed over the front and side entrances, all the back windows were barred, a pistol in a case lined with blue velvet lay on the dressing table of the guest room – it was loaded, we were warned – and a policeman stood day and night on duty at the corner. At the back of the house the cranes of the docks could be seen rising in the distance beyond a sea of rooftops, between which, from time to time, the funnels of a steamer moved out to Belfast Lough with a weary moan. From York Street, as it was then, cobbled side streets branched out with rows of small brick houses, built about the middle of the nineteenth century. They had names like Earl Street and Queen Street, but here lived no earls and queens, only the wretched and filthy poor. There were Protestant streets and Catholic streets distinguishable by their graffiti. Protestant walls were decorated with large, coloured murals of King William of Orange on a white horse, winning the Battle of the Boyne against Catholic James I. 'Remember 1690!' was the slogan and sometimes, rudely, 'Kick the Pope!' The Catholics retorted with a reminder of the Easter Uprising in Dublin, 'Remember 1916!' and 'Up Dev!' De Valera was then president of the Republic.[1] When Gallaher's factory siren sounded in the morning, a crowd of pale women, already gathered at the entrance, swarmed inside. They wore shawls round their shoulders and over their heads, sometimes a man's cap on their red or black hair as well. It was the time of the industrial depression between the two World Wars and unemployment was widespread. Men without jobs stood, year in, year out, at the corner of the factory, chewing tobacco and spraying a semicircle of rainbow-coloured spits on the pavement.

York Street was then a busy road from the centre of the city. Along this route marched the much-loved processions – Orangemen with black bowler hats and swinging orange sashes, the Irish guards in green tartan kilts, playing the bagpipes, and the Boys Brigade with their lively flutes – one of them must have been the later famous James Galway. When we heard the sound of music we used to run to the windows, where we had an excellent grandstand view. Sometimes the Lambeggers took up position on the street corner opposite. These were three men with big, black-covered drums, which they beat hour after hour in a monotonous, threatening rhythm. It was meant to strike fear into the hearts of the Catholics who lived a street or two away. The ominous sound scared us too. When there were riots, we lay in our beds with brass bedsteads and listened to angry voices quarrelling below. The tall trams did not stop in our street then but went clanging and swaying hurriedly past. 'It's all right, there is a policeman guarding our house!' soothed our mother.

In the street we watched 'the dirty children' play. We were wistful and envious because we were not allowed to join them. They had bugs and diseases, we were told. Sometimes they looked up at us, our noses flattened on the windowpane, and made rude faces. There was little traffic on the side streets then and they were free for ball games, a hopscotch and spinning tops. In the spring the May Queens emerged, a relic of English village life in the seventeenth century. Groups of children, singing and dancing, accompanied their May Queen, who wore a paper crown and coloured paper garments. They sang the praises of their queen: 'Our queen can burl her leg, burl her leg ...' 'Our queen will never die ...' and other verses which I have forgotten. When two such groups met there was a battle. The May Queen processions, like some other customs of the seventeenth century, lasted longer in Ireland than in England.

As we were not allowed to play in the street, we could play freely in the house. Our playroom was sparsely furnished, with linoleum on the floor, a bare wooden table, an old bank cupboard for toys and three curtainless windows with a bleak view of Gallaher's Tobacco factory opposite. There was decorative coloured wallpaper, on which three Japanese ladies with sunshades recurred regularly among winding creepers. We were not confined to this room, however, and on Sundays our playground was the bank office. There can hardly be a finer playground. We roller-skated among the marble pillars, slid along the polished counter and played house in the small compartments for the office staff. We also hurtled down the stairs on a big tin tray as a toboggan and must have made a great noise because once our policeman guard complained that a crowd had collected, thinking that a robbery was in progress. On fine days we were taken for walks on the bare heathery mountains which surround Belfast or took the train to the seaside in Whitehead. We were all members of the Belfast Naturalists' Field Club, which provided botanical and geological excursions.

'Now wash your hands and tidy yourselves!' When we were unexpectedly told this just after lunch, we were thrown into a state of excitement because it meant that we were going to a theatre matinee. I well remember my first visit. It was to see *A Midsummer Night's Dream*, a lavish Frank Benson production in Reinhardt[2] style, and my addiction to the theatre was founded. We went to the pantomime too and saw *Jack and the Beanstalk*, a family of giants clowning and thumping their way over the stage on stilts.

Only the cinema was not allowed, because it was considered vulgar and attended by an audience with infectious diseases, not to mention the bugs. So the only pictures we saw were the Medici prints of Dutch and Italian painters, which hung on the walls of our home. Sometimes, when it was raining, we went to church in St Anne's Cathedral, where we had all been baptized, and occasionally we were visited by the curate. My father was very sociable, as people are in the west of Ireland, and his ordered life included bridge parties. Then the small green card tables were set up and tea was served in the ornate silver tea service, which had been a wedding present, accompanied by sandwiches and cake. There was no alcohol in the house. As a boy my father used to be sent to fetch Grandfather Shaw home from the hotels of Manorhamilton, where he sat drinking and playing cards. This led my father to join the temperance movement, and he 'took the Pledge' in a public rally at the age of nine, Grandfather Shaw encouraged him, however, to take a hand at the game of bridge, and he became an excellent player. We led a varied and interesting life inside the four walls of our house, but it could not escape us that life outside was grim. The poverty of the ragged poor, the barefoot, half-naked children playing in the gutter. Once, sitting opposite an old woman in the tram, her shawl fell apart, revealing skinny, bare brown ribs. All this left a lasting impression of human suffering, of social injustice, that all was far from well. Every evening crowds gathered at the harbour to sing sad songs and wave goodbye to their relatives, leaving on the steamers to England and Scotland, in search of work and a better life.

7

O'Donnell Abú

Proudly the note of the trumpet is sounding,
Loudly the war-cries arise on the gale;
Fleetly the steed by Lough Swilly is bounding,
To join the thick squadrons in Saimer's green vale.
On ev'ry mountaineer,
Strangers to flight and fear!
Rush to the standard of dauntless Red Hugh!
Bonnaught and gallowglass,
Throng from each mountain pass;
On for old Erin, 'O'Donnell Abú !'

Michael Joseph McCann, 1824–1883

On St Patrick's Day, 17 March, my father divided up a little bunch of shamrock, the national symbol of Ireland, and gave each of us a sprig to put in our hatbands or buttonholes. This did not seem unusual then, but thinking back, it seems strange that we in the North wore 'the green', symbol of rebellion, once punishable by death.[1]

My father was born in 1870 and was already a young man when Parnell, 'the uncrowned king of Ireland', died. Parnell led the campaign for the independence of Ireland from Britain, until in 1890 the scandal of his divorce and marriage to Kitty O'Shea cost him job and influence.[2]

In 1968 I was sitting in a bar in London, discussing the disturbances in Ireland with one of my brothers, when the Irish barmaid interrupted, 'If it had not been for Kitty O'Shea,' she said, 'the whole history of Ireland would have been different!' This affair reduced the interest of many in day-to-day politics. However, my father bought a book about the history of Ireland by W.F. Collier on 26 April 1898, as he noted in his spidery hand on the flyleaf. W.F. Collier was once headmaster of the Belfast Royal Academy, the co-educational school I attended from 1924 until 1933. The boys wore red and blue caps with a badge in front. We girls wore navy-blue tunics with white blouses, long black stockings and hats with a wide brim, a red and blue ribbon and a badge. When there were riots we took the tram to school, rather than walk through the streets where the poor lived, because our school uniform identified us too strongly as Protestant middle class.

I was four when I first went to school. My sister Matilda had reached the compulsory school age of five, and our mother felt that I might as well go along too. We were as inseparable as twins. I was proud and amazed at the speed with which my sister learned to read aloud, and when at the end of the first year she was moved up into the second class and I was not, I felt like a terrible dunce, and I can still see the scratched desk on which I laid my head and wept, refusing to be comforted by our kindly teacher, Miss McVeigh. It was the first time that I had been parted from my sister. We still walked to school together and met afterwards to go home – down Hillman Street, Protestant, or Meadow Street, Catholic, across North Queen Street, Catholic, and down Earl Street, Protestant, to York Street.

Sister Matilda and Elizabeth in Whitehead, County Antrim, 1924.

The Academy was a grey granite building in the style of a Scottish castle, with a turret at each end and a wide flight of steps in the middle, leading up to the front entrance. It had been founded in 1795. The influence of the French Revolution and the American War of Independence resulted in Ireland in the movement known as the United Irishmen, led by Wolfe Tone, who was later executed by the British.[3] He represented the liberal-minded Protestants of the North. The Academy was founded in a republican spirit of enlightenment and tolerance – the 'Royal' was added much later. In my time the headmaster was A.R. Foster, who directed the school very much in the tradition of its founders. He was very young then, but as children see their teachers, he was ageless, very thin, with deep furrows in his cheeks. Foster was married to the sister of Robert Lynd, a left-wing writer, and they had one daughter, Christine, who later married Conor Cruise O'Brien. The Fosters had an adopted daughter as well, the granddaughter of Sir Samuel Ferguson, national poet and collector of ancient Irish legends.

Our parents became good friends with the Fosters, and they often played the old Scottish game of golf together. The golf course was on the outskirts of Belfast, with a fine view over the sea. Behind the golf course rose the Cave Hill. On its rocky summit, known as Mc Art's Fort, Wolfe Tone and the United Irishmen had sworn an oath to free Ireland together.

Much later, in the sixties, Alec Foster was one of the founders of the 'Wolfe Tone Society', an organization which contributed much to the civil rights movement.

Foster was influenced by the Gaelic League, and introduced Irish as well as English history into the school curriculum. The blue eyes of Miss Elvidge, the Irish history teacher, flashed as she recounted to us the brutalities of the British in Ireland. We learned Irish folk dancing as well, which was unusual in Protestant schools. However, the curriculum was not entirely insular, for we learned free rhythmic dancing in the style of then fashionable Isadora Duncan, wearing short green cotton tunics in Grecian fashion. French plays in the original language, as well as Shakespeare, were performed under the trees in the playground.

At the head of the French department was an excitable French Madame, who was assisted by Mr Hugh O'Donnell, who came from the west of Ireland. Mr O'Donnell was smallish and slender, with thin hair on an egg-shaped head, glasses set on a hooky nose and a shy smile. He was full of fun and liked flirting with us girls. He had the classroom adjoining Madame, and when she could no longer control her unruly pupils, she would burst in, wringing her hands and tearfully appealing to him for help. He, peaceable man, was probably only able to soothe her and her class, because having managed to bring Madame to the peak of desperation, the pupils were willing to desist from teasing. 'Do you know,' said my father to A.R. Foster one day when they were playing golf, 'that you have the head of the O'Donnell clan on your French staff?' The O'Donnells were one of the great Irish Celtic tribes, and the headmaster was delighted to hear this and gave instructions at once that the battle hymn of the clan, 'O'Donnell Abú!', should be taught in the singing class. So its wild music rang out, shaking the windows of this respectable Presbyterian neighbourhood.

The teaching of English literature, languages and the arts was on a high level in the Academy, but the sciences were only formally represented. There was a laboratory, and a subject vaguely called 'Science' taught by Mr Carpenter, a Welshman with a big black moustache and a grand singing voice. He used to perform at school concerts, and I suspect that this is why he was engaged by Foster, who enjoyed singing himself. Mr Carpenter's interest in teaching was slight, and we had a splendid time vaulting over the laboratory desks during his lessons.

We had no religious education, but at the commencement of morning assembly in the gymnasium a chapter of the Bible was read, and a morning prayer was said, during which we remained standing, Presbyterian fashion. Madame and Mr O'Donnell, who were Catholics, and the few Jewish pupils waited outside until the prayer was over and then came in for announcements. So we learned to respect other beliefs.

Like all schools, the Academy smelt of chalk, wood and ink, with a sprinkling of old sandwich crumbs. What with computers and ballpoint pens, they probably smell differently today. When the janitor swung the big brass bell to announce the end of the school day, the pupils thundered wildly down the stairs, without any kind of order. Only the little ones were kept back in the classroom, so that they would not be trampled underfoot.

Our headmaster was a temperamental man, and sometimes flew into a rage when his veins swelled, and his blue eyes flashed in a terrifying fashion. In a state of wrath, he was prone to rash action. Once my brother Patrick innocently presented him with a note from our mother, excusing his absence from school the previous afternoon, because she had taken us to a theatre matinee to see a piece by Shakespeare. We had all been to it, of course, but my sister and I knew better than to give up our notes. Patrick was told harshly that he was expelled from the school, so he took his cap and went off, but he had hardly arrived home with the news than he was followed by the school janitor and the message that all was forgiven, he should return at once.

I remember my schooldays at the Academy as a happy time. It was a second home in which we grew from the sandpit to puberty in a climate of tolerance, liberalism and pleasant disorder. There was of course the fussy little teacher of domestic science, as sewing and cookery lessons were called, who always found fault with me, and the sadistic gymnastic teacher, but their misdeeds have faded away. There was an advisory committee of parents and teachers, and methods and aims of the headmaster led to many arguments, but there is no doubt that the influence of a dedicated pedagogue is of immense value, and this was in the end taken into account.

Then my father decided to retire from the bank and leave Belfast, which he had never liked anyway. My parents considered where they should move to – New Zealand, where several Shaw relatives were living? It was reported to be a beautiful and healthy country, but it was too far away. There was another brother in Dublin, but my mother protested that Irish was a compulsory subject in the schools there, and we would be at a disadvantage, not having studied the subject before. In the end they decided to move to England, and chose the small town of Bedford, with good, cheap schools and only fifty miles from London.

And so we left Ireland. 'For the whole country is going to pot!' said my father.

Monument to the Catholic priest Peter O' Neill
and his participation in the 1798 Rebellion. Memorial Park,
Youghal, Ireland, 1981.

II

I

The Search

... It was a hard responsibility to be a stranger,
to hear your speech sounding at odds with your
    neighbours;
holding your tongue from quick comparisons,
remembering that you are a guest in the house.

Often you will regret the voyage,
wakening in the dark night to recall that other place
or glimpsing the moon rising and recollecting
that it is also rising over named hills,
shining on known waters ...

John Hewitt, 1907–1987

Our parents bought a small, rather poky house near Bedford Station without seeing it first, because the price was right. It was semi-detached with a small stretch of garden between brick walls at the back. This was a great pleasure to us, never having had a garden of our own, and my mother and sister were endlessly designing new flower beds and borders and putting up trellises for roses and climbing plants. Bedford was then a small sleepy town, market centre of Bedfordshire, famous for its prison, where John Bunyan had written *The Pilgrim's Progress* in the seventeenth century. There were several good schools founded by the Harpur Trust, which offered reasonably priced education of a high standard, and therefore a great number of retired Indian Army or Civil Service settled there or sent their families to reside in Bedford during periods of overseas service.

There was a bookshop in the centre of town, which used to buy up libraries from country houses in the district and offer them for sale in their second-hand department, without much knowledge of their value, so I used to rummage about there and picked up some treasures, like books illustrated by Bewick,[1] for a few shillings saved from my pocket money.

I did not like Bedford. I did not like the flat agricultural landscape with the slow Ouse flowing through it, nor the dull little town, nor the Girls High School with its maiden teachers, hair strained back, beetling brows and glasses, large feet in heavy walking shoes. In those days women who married had to leave the profession, and this meant that those who stayed were usually plain.

In puberty, young people are inclined to see their elders as caricatures. In fact, this was a heroic generation of women who taught us. They had fought for the right of women to study at the universities; had been suffragettes fighting for the right for women to vote. Many had lost their possible husbands in the massive slaughter of the First World War.

When we changed countries and changed our school, we changed our school uniform too. In Bedford High School the uniform consisted of pastel-coloured blouses, navy tunics and brown stockings, and our mother asked the headmistress for permission that my sister and I could wear out our mountain of black stockings before we changed to brown. So at morning assembly there were 598 girls with brown stockings and two with black. We were marked as newcomers, but even when we refused to wear those black stockings, our accents and habits stamped us as outsiders.

My two brothers attended Bedford School, a minor public school for boys, which contrasted even more from the dear old Academy, being extremely conservative and traditional. I was homesick for Ireland, the landscape, the voices. I wept dramatically, bought books on the Irish language and wrote sentimental, nationalistic poems, still fired by the burning eyes of Miss Elvidge. I did not even try to catch up with the new subjects, such as chemistry and the Holy Scriptures, and was unresponsive to the two nice little girls who had been allocated to look after me.

After a year had passed, I gradually accustomed myself to the change, but the general restlessness of puberty increased. I could hardly wait to get away from home and school and was not nice to my long-suffering parents. But there were enjoyable times in Bedford too. We rode about the countryside on bicycles, visited London theatres, where we saw the Shakespeare plays that we were studying at school and noted with delight that Gielgud wept real tears in *Richard II*. We visited art exhibitions, among others a wonderful and unforgettable exhibition of Chinese art in the Royal Academy.

The cinema had become respectable, and we could go in the holidays, although the school did not allow it in term time. I had a girlfriend to whom someone once said that she looked like Greta Garbo, and this turned her head so much that her one wish – which came true – was to go on the stage. We would sit through three continuous performances in the cinema, as if we were drugged, and spent hours dreamily browsing through film magazines, completely hooked on the Hollywood fairytale. We began to catch up with the media too. On our newly acquired radio set, we heard news of unrest in Europe, of the Nazis taking over in Germany, war in Abyssinia and Spain. News which made us uneasy, but still seemed remote and unreal. At the end of 1936 my sister and I went to Paris for a month. It must have cost our parents a fortune. We stayed in the fashionable suburb of Neuilly, near the Bois de Boulogne, in the apartment of Madame de Troudon, who took in English girls who should improve their French. There was a governess who gave us lessons every morning and took us on sight-seeing tours. Madame de Troudon was a Royalist and, on the walls, hung portraits of her noble ancestors. She had two daughters, who inquired when we would be presented at court, and when they heard that this was not to be, lost interest in us at once. On the lavatory door hung a poster of the extreme right-wing 'Croix de Feu'. Madame made no secret of her support for the Nazis in Germany and insisted that the Soviet Union was the real enemy of France. On the coffee table in the salon, furnished with elegant furniture in the style of Louis XV, lay leaflets with crude-coloured drawings of hanged Bolsheviks. All this made my sister, who was reading Tolstoy, very unhappy and every evening in our bedroom I would assure her that we would go home tomorrow and made comforting remarks until there was a banging on the thin wall and a shout of '*Parlez Francais!*'

We were supposed to never speak a word of English – well meant, of course. My sister had already spent a month in France, staying with a friendly potter's family, but for me it was the first time I had been outside the British Isles, and I found it wildly exciting. In those days there were trams in Paris, with little platforms on the end on which we used to stand and relish that wonderful foreign smell of garlic – a scent which always reminds me of that first exotic trip abroad. We visited the Louvre and saw the blue windows of Notre Dame. We went to see Corneille's *Le Cid,* performed in classical style, and *Le Malade Imaginaire* by Molière, with the decor by Christian Berard. We were taken to Versailles too, of course, Madame conducted us personally, rebuked us for not walking straight, and observed us with a cold blue eye, just as she did when we did not know what to do with the finger bowls at dinner.

For me it was an unforgettable trip and we got good marks in our French exams.

2

'Der Krieg soll verflucht sein.' ['War be damned.']
Mutter Courage und ihre Kinder [Mother Courage and her Children]

Bertolt Brecht

I am told that when I was four I already announced that I would be an artist, probably prompted by my mother, who used to draw pictures for us. I liked watching her hesitant pencil line, but then she noticed that my sister and I were drawing the back legs of a chair as well as the front and she gave up. We drew pictures and pinned them up on the walls of our playroom. Once we took part in a drawing competition run by a newspaper and my sister Matilda won a prize, but I did not, which made me secretly very huffy.

The art teacher at the Academy praised my imagination and encouraged me. None of the drawings of that time have been preserved. When I learned to read and write, I wrote little pieces of prose and poetry for *The Owl*, the school magazine, and was praised and encouraged by Mr Shearman, the head of the English department. In my second school, in England, I again did well in drawing, history and English literature. I loved poetry and could learn it by heart very rapidly. In the drawing class I soon became Miss Beck's favourite pupil, and in the afternoon she gave me a little private tuition. She outlined a glowing career for me. I should go to art school in London for three years, then on to the Royal College, then I should win the Rome Prize and ascend to undefined clouds of glory. This was shortly before the School Certificate examination and it was time to decide on a career. I would have liked to go to the university and study history, but my marks were very uneven – hopeless in mathematics, for instance. A general high standard was required for exemption from matriculation, university entrance, and the teachers thought I was unlikely to achieve this. To the surprise of everyone I managed to pass in all subjects and received a curious document stating that on the payment of five pounds I could receive a certificate giving me the necessary exemption. Five pounds was a lot of money in those days, so I just kept the letter.

A university career would have meant another two years at school – and in Bedford – so I went to the Chelsea Art School in London,[1] where one of Miss Beck's former pupils was a student.

'Don't', said my mother, 'ever eat those big blocks of dates you see in Miss Boye's shop, because they have been trampled flat by Arabs with bare feet and big dirty toenails!' This was just one of the few pieces of unworldly and colourful advice with which she hoped to equip us for life.

'Don't', she said, when at the age of seventeen I left home to study at Chelsea School of Art, 'don't ever pick up a handkerchief dropped by an old lady. It may be chloroformed, and you would fall down unconscious and wake up as a white slave in South America!'

Fitted out with a new tweed jacket and skirt, as well as what was then known as an afternoon dress and an awful frizzy permanent wave beneath which I still wore my horn-rimmed spectacles, I set out to explore London and life. My parents had arranged for me to stay in a boarding house for girls, recommended by an old Irish cousin, but I soon moved out of that.

London – big city smells, petrol, straw and dust, the rattle and roar of traffic, reminiscent of Belfast. Not like small-town Bedford, the past four years of ordered girls' school, the pressures of puberty upon us. Bedford, closed-in, safe, retired colonels, ladies on bicycles, almond blossom in the front gardens. Can't breathe. No vision. London, London offers all. On the first day in art school I was put in the life class. We sat in a circle on so-called wooden donkeys round the model and the teacher, the painter Robert

Medley, hovered round and explained to me how to construct a figure with a few basic lines. When I looked at the drawings the other students had done, it seemed to me that in comparison I was hopelessly incapable. I was on the verge of tears. Like others who have been teacher's pet, best-in-the-class, previously, I suffered when I discovered that I was just one of many. On my way back to my dismal boarding house, I remember that I went into a café and consoled myself with a large piece of chocolate cake and the sympathetic glance of the friendly waitress.

I was not convinced for quite a long time that I should be studying art, but my parents maintained that having decided on this career, I should stick to it. I attended the art classes half-heartedly, and spent much time wandering about London. Every week I examined the advertisements in the *New Statesman*, which listed cultural events, and went on voyages of exploration, looking for a star. I walked along the Thames Embankment, upon Westminster Bridge, and into the City. I heard Professor Joad[2] speak to the Peace Pledge Union – we all knew that war was coming – and saw T.S. Eliot's *Murder in the Cathedral* performed in a city church. Eliot's poetry fascinated me and his severe, pessimistic and sonorous tones echoed constantly in my mind. I often went to meetings at Conway Hall in Red Lion Square, Holborn, which was rented out to various liberal causes. As I sat there listening to talk of impending war, I read the quotation which was displayed in large gold letters above the platform – 'To thine own self be true' – and wondered what it meant. Not long ago I passed it again and saw a small statue of a man still living then, the ninety-year-old pacifist Fenner Brockway, with baggy trousers and spectacles, just as he looked when I heard him speak, many years before. It had been erected in the square. I looked into the hall, the same but a little shabbier, and the same quotation still stood above the platform, and I wondered again what it meant.

One day in 1939 I gatecrashed the private view of an exhibition of the work of Amédée Ozenfant, who was on his way from Paris to New York. He was one of the leading avant-garde artists and a publicist of the modern movement at that time. He invented the movement known as Purism and edited with Le Corbusier the magazine called *L'Esprit Nouveau* in

Paris. The exhibition was opened by Herbert Read, quiet and restrained in contrast to the vivacious artist. Read's *The Meaning of Art* was my introduction to modern art in my schooldays, now I bought Ozenfant's orange book, *Foundations of Modern Art* and read it avidly. He wrote, 'Never forget to look up at the stars!'

Ah stars. I lost the book long since, but I still look up when I remember.

3

On my excursions through London I was alone, but I made some friends among the girls at art school, as well as in my lodgings, which I often changed. I used to play tennis with the son of my landlady in number 11 Cheyne Row, and there I got to know a lady who worked as a private secretary to a businessman and divulged all the details of her sex life with him, which I found very interesting. We all ate dinner together in the evening: one of the lodgers was a psychiatrist who used us for various experimental tests, mostly with pencil and paper, then told us, with a secretive smile, which mental aberration would befall us should we become unbalanced. Our landlady charged me very little for this accommodation because she liked me as a companion for her son, but unfortunately she was killed in an air raid, when Chelsea Old Church, just opposite, was hit and she had gone there to take shelter in the crypt.

Remembering my mother's advice, I looked at old ladies with suspicion, but saw none drop a handkerchief. The elegant London men who wore bowler hats and striped trousers attracted my attention. The horn-rimmed spectacles were abandoned, so too the tweedy costume, and I acquired a black coat, a black hat with a veil, cream-coloured gloves and a cream umbrella. The suave look. Then one day, as I entered my lodgings, I was spoken to by a tall gentleman who said he was visiting friends there. He wore striped trousers, black jacket, black umbrella and a worldly manner. I was dazzled when he invited me to lunch, impressed when he presented himself as a journalist, surprised when I saw no books in his flat, and startled by his attempted seduction. Fellow students at art school told me later that he was a well-known jewel thief, operating mostly in the Burlington Arcade, and not even a very good one, for he had been arrested a few times. I abandoned my illusions, together with hat, veil and cream umbrella, adopted a woollen jersey and sandals. My perm grew out by itself.

The students at the Chelsea School of Art at that time consisted partly of young ladies of affluent families who were filling out the time between leaving school and marriage by taking up painting as an accomplishment. One had recently been presented at court and was busy doing a large watercolour painting of this event. There was a lovely blonde, who always wore some kind of beachwear which exposed her golden skin, and a little, dark girl of nineteen, always elegantly dressed, who was engaged to marry – to our horror – an old man of thirty. 'Nothing,' I remember her saying, as she washed her paintbrushes in the cloakroom, 'spoils that look of soignée like an untidy parcel.' This amazing thought had never occurred to me.

These self-assured and sophisticated young people gossiped gaily in the common room until from time to time they were chased out by gruff old George Day in his long white smock, dotted with paint. Attendance at the school was not checked. Paying students came and went as they liked. The non-paying students, who received grants from London County Council, had to complete certain courses and examinations and do a year of teacher training afterwards.

'Are you a serious student?' I was asked by small, bald-headed and rather peppery Brian Robb, assistant teacher in the class for book illustration. There were indeed serious students among the paying students too. There were a number of extremely gifted girls, but one heard little of them later. They seem to have dropped out under pressure of marriage and children. Prunella Clough was one of the few whose name I saw in art publications many years later, on my occasional visits to London. As a student she lived with an aunt in Sloane Square, and we used to walk home along the King's Road together. She was not at all one of the fashionable set, dreamy and unworldly, her skirts always the wrong length.

Among the young men was one whose dark eyes attracted my attention. Slight, agile and neat, he was always surrounded by pretty girls. His name was Dirk Bogarde, and he became a well-known actor and writer.

I began my studies by signing on for a general art course, which included life drawing, anatomy, perspective and drawing from antique plaster casts, which I enjoyed. The teacher for the last subject was Hugh Finney, who praised my drawings from the antique and showed an interest in my work, which is why I always attended his class on Thursdays instead of exploring London, which I otherwise did. In my second year I decided to concentrate on book illustration in the department led by Graham Sutherland. He was an excellent teacher. He had a monkish look, with his small dark head and candid blue eyes. Wearing a blue smock, he went quietly from one student to the other, examining their work. On the edge of the paper, he sometimes drew little sketches to suggest changes, and I wish I had preserved these delicate drawings.

I continued to attend the life class once a week. In his book *A Postillion Struck by Lightning*, Dirk Bogarde describes the models in the life class as 'always ugly, always thin or vastly fat, as unacceptable naked as they must have been fully clothed'. But I remember at least two models who did not meet this description at all. One was a young girl with a strong Maillol figure, who told us she could tear a telephone directory in two; the other was the model Wendy Blood, who later married the painter Victor Pasmore. She had an extraordinary blonde skin with a greenish tinge and looked as if she could have been a model for Renoir.

During my first year in the illustration class, I entered a competition for a scholarship, submitting illustrations for *Wuthering Heights* by Emily Brontë. I was not awarded the scholarship, but as I walked along the corridor next day I was approached by Henry Moore, who was the head of the sculpture department, and who told me that in the jury for the competition he and Graham Sutherland had both voted for me as the best candidate, and he had never seen such good illustrations to *Wuthering Heights*, and I should not be down-hearted. This encouragement from an artist I had long revered was better than any prize for me. In my euphoria I signed in for the evening class in sculpture, but found it taken by someone else and I was given a plaster ear to copy and my career as a sculptor lasted just one day. Henry Moore was a fairly young man then, small, compact and muscular. He was always modest and unassuming in his manner, although he was already famous through the appreciation of his work by the critic Herbert Read. In 1939 we had the last end-of-term fête before the war put an end to such events, when teachers and pupils used to perform for the amusement of others on a small stage. I remember Henry Moore and his assistant Hugh Finney delighted us with a ballet dance, both dressed in pink tights, with tiny pink rosettes as nipples, which they tore off at the end of the dance and flung at the audience. Henry Moore impressed us especially by leaping into the air and doing what I think is called a double salto.[1]

Henry Moore draws the A. T. S. (Auxiliary Territorial Service)
(*Our artists as war correspondents*).

When the war began, Moore was appointed an official War Artist and gave up teaching. Despite the British government policy of appeasing the Nazis, it was generally realized that war was inevitable. There had been horrifying accounts of war in Abyssinia and in Spain, photographs of bombardments and the distress of refugees, and military conflict spread over Europe and the Far East. Chamberlain's government vacillated in its opposition to Hitler and the Nazis. The Munich Agreement of 1938 between England, France and Germany had permitted the Nazis to march into Czechoslovakia and incorporate it into the German Reich. I remember the little Czech art student, my friend Anouska, was in tears during those days and would not speak to us because she thought we were indifferent to the fate of her country. Now it was clear that the Spanish Civil War was going to end in a victory for fascist Franco. There were those in the governments of Britain and France who – like Madame de Trudon – considered the Soviet Union to be the real enemy and were prepared to take no decision until Hitler turned his aggression towards the East, when they would be glad to give him support or at least witness the mutual destruction of both countries. As the governments wavered, a wide front of left-wing opposition grew and there were massive demonstrations calling for aid to the Spanish government and for a united antifascist opposition.

One day I found a leaflet in the common room, advertising a May Day demonstration against fascism, with the headline – a quotation from the Nazis – 'When I hear the word culture, I reach for my revolver!' I went along, out of sympathy and curiosity. The contingent of the art school included some of the teachers, including Henry Moore. I walked happily behind him as we chanted, 'Arms for Spain! Down the drain with Chamberlain!'

'Graham Sutherland covers the 2ND Front' (*Our artists as war correspondents*).

4

The communist students noted my presence and began to approach me as a possible recruit after that. One of the most active was Patrick Carpenter. I had noticed him earlier because of his odd appearance. Tall and thin, with an enormous forehead, black hair combed back and flattened in the fashion of the day, green eyes glinting behind his glasses and a proletarian, diffident slouch, he was no beauty. He had a wide mouth, uneven teeth and a scratchy cockney voice. He was very sure of himself and had his own style of painting, which had nothing to do with the trend set in the painting class by Graham Sutherland. At that time English painting tended towards a return to the romanticism of the early nineteenth century, to the tradition of Blake and Samuel Palmer. Pat painted large gloomy scenes of derelict buildings hung with coloured bunting, in the surrealist style. His pictures were intended to show a dreamlike vision of social decay. He had exhibited in the big London Surrealist Exhibition a year or two before when he was only sixteen and was immensely proud that his picture had been reproduced on the front page of the *Radio Times*.

I visited him in his parents' home in a place called World's End, on the western fringe of Chelsea. It was a tiny working-class house, two rooms up, two down, with a little yard at the back where his father grew a mass of flowers. He was a large, kindly man, a bus driver, if I remember rightly. Pat's mother was a merry, curly-haired cockney, who worked as a housekeeper for a rich old gent, and tapped his whiskey bottle for Pat, her only son. In his tiny, cell-like room upstairs, Pat's easel and large paintings stacked against the wall took up most of the space, a narrow bed against the other wall. Pat, with his doom and gloom, did not seem to resemble either of his parents, but there was something theatrical in his pronouncements when he proclaimed, for instance, 'We are orphans of the social storm!' which suggested a zest for life.

It was a time of acute confrontation between left and right. The star turned red for many. On reading the *Communist Manifesto* it seemed to me that all those troublesome and oppressive questions about social justice, which scenes in Belfast had raised for me, were adequately explained and a solution offered in the Marxist theory of the class struggle.

'But I don't like all this hate!' I said.

'You must learn to hate!' answered Pat, in his grimmest doom-and-gloom manner. He informed the comrades that I wished to join the Communist Artists Party Group, called the Hogarth Group, named after William Hogarth, the realistic painter of the nineteenth century, and the secretary called past to give me a card, without ceremony.

5

When war was declared in September 1939, the art school closed, as massive air attacks on London were anticipated. We students were on holiday then, but a little later, when it seemed that aerial bombing was not expected in England, the art school reopened with a diminished number of staff and students. I had begun to do a course of training as a voluntary nurse in Chelsea, but then returned to my art studies until the autumn of 1940, when the bombing of London began, what was known as the Blitz, Hitler's Blitzkrieg. When the Blitz began I was in London just for the day because the holidays were still on and I was staying in Bedford. Pat and I were walking in Hyde Park when the sky was suddenly filled with aeroplanes, and as we stared upwards, anti-aircraft guns went off in the park and startled us. A man who was passing on his bicycle and staring up too, fell off and lay there groaning, unable to get up. He must have hurt himself seriously and Pat was busy organizing an ambulance for the poor fellow, so that we were distracted from the event of the day until an air-raid warden hustled us into the entrance of a shelter. I took the train back to Bedford that evening, watching London in flames behind me. A burning sugar factory lit up the sky, visible for many miles away. I was informed that the art school would not reopen till further notice.

Not knowing what to do in the meantime, I went fruit-picking in Cambridgeshire, together with a number of other students in the same position. We slept in a barn and went out to the orchard to work in those beautiful, calm September mornings. On Fridays we were handed a modest pay packet – my first earnings. Then Pat wrote to suggest that we take a flat in London together. He had a job in the communist *Daily Worker* as caricaturist and could support us. We took a mews flat in Richmond because we thought it was out of reach of the air attacks. One could rent a flat in Park Lane for almost nothing in those days because the wealthy had taken off for the country. Richmond was an elegant area too, but our mews flat did not cost much. I had a problem getting there from Bedford because the main stations in London were bombed and out of use, and I had to go round the city's devious bus routes. I met Pat in Ealing and we spent the first night staying with a friend there, all three sleeping under a steel table, which was a government issue air-raid protection.

In Richmond, Pat travelled by rail to the *Daily Worker* office every day and back again, putting a little E in the corner of his cartoons for me. I played housewife and waited for his return in the evening. We had thought Richmond would be a quiet place but every evening the guns in the park went off, shrapnel rained down, and our little mews flat, built on stilts so to speak, shook and trembled. We lay in bed, clasping each other and shaking too. Before Pat returned in the evening, I felt uneasy when the guns started up, thinking of him walking back from the station through the air raid, and would sit, a little scared, alone under the kitchen table till he came. But then we would sometimes go out and dance in the empty moonlit street together because we were so totally romantic, daring the fates, as we thought. This all lasted only about six weeks. Then one day a telegram came to inform Pat that he was called up to the army and should report the next day at two o'clock in the morning in Liverpool Street Station. Troop trains left at night. The telegram had been delayed because it had been sent to his parents' house at World's End first. We went there the next day to collect a few belongings, and I took his father's tin hat – his steel helmet – along. The parents were not there. They slept elsewhere because of the bombing. We took the last underground train to Liverpool Street, and stood in the darkened station among shadowy people, embracing each other and waiting for departure time. Then slowly the train slid off into the blackness and Pat was gone. I went out of the station, put on the tin hat and set out for home on foot, as there was no more public transport. I did not mind a long walk. Then as now, I enjoyed walking through my beloved London. The moon shone brightly. One could be fairly sure that there would be an air raid, but I thought I'd dive down somewhere if necessary.

When I go through the city today and see the dense and noisy traffic, people rushing to and fro, all haste, indifference and stress, it is hard to believe in the reality of that night in 1940. The street outside the station was empty of traffic, as indeed were all the streets. It was absolutely silent. The massive bank buildings threw great dark shadows. I walked in the middle of the road, and there was no sound except my echoing footsteps. I went past St Paul's Cathedral. There was no living being to be seen, not even a cat. In Ludgate Hill and Fleet Street there was dead silence, hushed emptiness. It was as if I was the only living person in London, a singular loneliness, exciting too, as if I was the sole survivor of some great catastrophe. It was the dreamlike emptiness of surrealism. Pat's ominous pictures had become reality. As I went down Aldgate and the Strand, the sun rose, the sky turned pale blue, and the houses were lit with a soft pink and yellow light. When I reached Trafalgar Square, I met a human being. It was an air-raid warden, standing in the middle of the street and he stared at me as I approached, long hair streaming from under my tin hat. 'Where did you spring from?' he asked, looking as if he had seen a ghost, and I was back in the world of men. I walked on, through Green Park, Hyde Park and Kensington Gardens to Chelsea, where I deposited the tin hat at World's End and took the train back to Richmond.

There I laid my head on Pat's leather jacket and wept a little. I did not want to sleep alone in the shuddering mews flat and so I went to the cellar of an empty house at the back, where the landlady had laid out mattresses and told us we could sleep if we liked. When she found me there alone the next night, however, she insisted that I spend the nights in her cellar. There were several people there, one of whom continually hummed and directed an imaginary orchestra. A few days later there was a firebomb attack on Richmond. We all ran around with pails of water. A small bomb fell on the house opposite, while I was standing at the door, and my eardrum burst in the blast. When an infection developed, because of the dust raised, I was advised by the doctor to leave London in case I should need hospital treatment as the London hospitals were reserved for bomb casualties and were also targets. There was no sense in staying in London now anyway, so I packed my bags and returned to Bedford.

I visited Pat a few times on the south coast where he was stationed and where a German invasion was expected. Ramsgate and Dover were almost completely evacuated and civilians entering the area were checked. Grass grew in the streets and the houses were empty or occupied by the military. The towns were being shelled from the French coast. The military police were nice to girls visiting soldiers and let me pass through. On the quay at Ramsgate we stood with a group of onlookers and watched a shot-down German plane sink in the sea, the pilot on top of the wreckage waving for help. No one went to his rescue. Hate ruled. I got to know the nice young men with whom Pat was friendly in the army. Jimmy was killed in El Alamein. Robert in Monte Cassino. Pat went on the long journey with Montgomery's Eighth Army through North Africa and Italy. At the end of the war he was in Vienna, and wrote to me from there about the wonderful Breughels he had seen. He wrote to me during all the six years of his soldiering, even though he knew we were no longer together in the way we used to be. When he came back he took a job as a teacher in a London art school, and painted again too. But the paintings I saw no longer showed that rare certainty of vision. His romanticism did not survive the war. Around 1956, after the uprising in Hungary, he left the Communist Party. We still wrote to each other after the war and met occasionally when I was in England. He married a Polish girl. As time passed the contact grew less. Recently a visitor told me he had died two years before. I don't know where or why. He was not very old. I was shocked, and suddenly I felt a great silence and loneliness around me, like that time when we were separated and I walked back through an empty city, so reminiscent of his early foreboding and visionary paintings. I have one still, which he painted for my nineteenth birthday. It shows a dark and desolate landscape, decayed wooden hoardings with peeling shreds of paper. On the right three small figures are running away into a bare wasteland, in the foreground two small boys whisper to each other. In the middle is a ruined house, Pat and I standing hesitantly in front of it. Pat indicates something, his arm slightly raised. I hold his arm as if in restraint. A light evening sky behind darkening buildings.

Maybe having this picture makes me always feel his presence and reminds me of our brief, innocent and happy time together.

Poster, 1942.

6

When I returned to Bedford to nurse my ear, I was uncertain what to do next. Eventually I expected to be called up for national service. When I heard that what was left of the municipal London art schools were to reopen, merged in one school with a reduced number of teachers, in the Midlands town of Northampton, I decided to carry on with my studies and went there to look for accommodation. The art school had a list of addresses and I was given lodgings in a little brick house, the home of an old Midlands family, dwarfed because of generations of underfeeding, enthusiastic members of the Independent Labour Party, who received me kindly.

The art school functioned half-heartedly in the town polytechnic. Those students who were there either waited for call-up or were registered pacifists. The entire family of the architect Clough Williams-Ellis had taken up residence in Northampton, so too the musicians Malcolm Arnold and Richard Adeney, whose sister Charlotte was studying painting. Parties and gatherings were organized, but somehow the bohemian atmosphere of Soho did not fit into this old industrial town. I very often cycled to Bedford at weekends, through the pretty grey stone villages. Nice flat country for cycling. One night I dreamt of the bombing in London and seemed to hear the thud of bombs all night. In the morning I heard that Coventry, about twenty miles away, had been almost razed to the ground.

Northampton seemed to me a backwater, and after Christmas I decided to go back to London and look for a job. I took an empty room in Fellowes Road, Hampstead, furnished it with a bedstead and three wooden boxes, one to sit on, one for a table and one to put things in. I found a job painting dolls' faces in a small factory in Willesden, where a girlfriend was already working. I only worked four days a week, and was paid two pounds, which was enough to live on and left time to do something else. It was a small sweatshop. They brought in a tray of bald dolls heads, on which we were required to paint mouth, eyes and two spots for the nostrils. If I was tempted to vary the expression, a slight smile on the lips for instance, it was sent back. When the heads ran out, we stuffed teddy bears. There was one woman there who had been doing this for ten years, which seemed to me to be an unbelievably long time to have tolerated the squalid and dreary building and the drudgery and boredom of the work. When I asked her why she put up with it, she replied that she had always been afraid that she would not get another job.

After about six weeks I had had enough, and took a job in Camden Town, where I was then living. I earned ten shillings more and it was just round the corner. It was a firm called Cinema Signs, which provided posters for weekly cinema programmes. I used to leap out of bed at the last moment, go round to the factory and clock in, then go out again to have breakfast in a small workers' café until the manager noticed and politely requested me to stay on the premises. We had two tea breaks, one in the morning when we were allowed to sit, and one in the afternoon when we were supposed to drink it standing. The manager was then always popping in suddenly, hoping to catch one of us sitting. Our foreman, Julius, taught me the art of signwriting, and when I could draw a perfect O with one sweep of the brush, I was allowed to begin seriously. Apart from Julius, there was a handsome but spotty boy of sixteen, a couple of deaf mutes and a man whose name I have forgotten, who was an anarchist and had been a member of the International Brigade in Spain. He showed me leaflets and pamphlets with photos of former members of the Soviet leadership, believed to have been murdered by Stalin. I rejected the allegations immediately. I did not like his mean face and anyway what one does not want to know falls on deaf ears.

At this time, I lived in Camden Studios. I had taken over the studio from an artist who had been called up into the army. There were six studios facing each other, with a scrubby patch of garden in the middle. Opposite me lived Cliff Rowe, a communist artist, one of the founders of the Artists International Association. He became a dear friend, honest and incorruptible, humorous and warm-hearted. Basically, he was a lone wolf, but he had numerous affairs with women. When I first met him he was living with the writer Edith Simon, but then he fell in love with a young blonde girl called Doris, who worked at Carreras Tobacco Factory in Mornington Crescent. In the next studio to mine worked the Hungarian sculptor, Peter (Lazlo) Peri, who had fled from persecution from Hungary and then from Berlin. He belonged to the avant-garde of the twenties in Europe and was a contributor to Herwarth Walden's *Der Sturm*.[1] He worked in coloured concrete, at first in the constructivist manner, then he turned later to figurative art. While I was living in Camden Studios, Peri made a large head of Stalin, black moustache and all; it was very heavy, and we all helped to carry it to the lorry when he submitted it to the jury of an exhibition and carried it back again when it was rejected. We did not understand anything about the constructivist movement at that time and considered Peri, and his impassioned speeches in terrible English at artists' meetings, light entertainment. He was tolerant of our lack of understanding. Later he found a promoter in the art critic John Berger, and my friend John Hewitt bought several of his works for the Herbert Art Gallery in Coventry, when he was director there. Now his work is represented in major collections, in London and in Hungary. In 1982 I saw a banner stretched across the pavement in West Berlin, advertising an exhibition in the Kunsthalle of Lazlo Peri. He would have been pleased.

I think I last saw Peri at some exhibition in the late fifties. He ran towards me, arms outstretched, tears in his eyes, to tell me that his wife had left him. This Central European told me that I should stay in England, not go back to Germany. When I said in my innocence, that I thought I was needed there, he replied with a wave of they hand, 'The Germans always need you!'

7

In the thirties and forties, the right-wing fascist movements which were in power in Germany and Italy had parallels in all European countries including England, France and Spain. The left–right confrontation reached a peak at the outbreak of the Spanish Civil War. We young people of that time felt bound to take sides – after all, we were the ones who would be called on to fight in a war – and it seemed as if a determined front against fascism might check its spread now. The International Brigade was formed to aid the Spanish government against the onslaught by Franco and his Nazi supporters. Many of the volunteers from different countries gave their lives in its ranks.

I forgot about dreamy Irish nationalism and was fired instead by the ideals and hopes of a generation that aimed at an international society, which would put an end to war and social injustice. We fervently believed that the experiment in a different social order, which was taking place in the Soviet Union, was the hope of the world. When war finally broke out in 1939, the Comintern in Moscow – the committee which issued directives to the national communist parties – announced that this was not a real war against fascism because of the lukewarm attitude of the British and French government, and sent out a call for all people, including the Germans, to overthrow their governments and unite for peace. In England an organization called 'The People's Convention' was formed but faded away in the course of the war. Its Cultural Committee, however, drew together a wide number of people of various shades of opinion – communists, pacifists and liberals. There were readings, discussions and musical evenings. The musicians Ben Frankel and Van Phillips played us the latest jazz records they had received from America, and we were enriched by contact with various aspects of cultural life, and the people concerned with it.

Peter and the Wolf.

Peter and the Wolf.

We often met in the evening in the basement restaurant of Lyons Corner House in Oxford Street, which was open all night during the bombing. There I got to know Alexander Mackendrick. He was working then with John Halas in Batchelor Cartoon Films, and he told me a little about cartoon film-making. He arranged a showing in a cinema of drawings I had done for *Peter and the Wolf* to accompany the music of Prokofiev. Mackendrick was tall and handsome with wide shoulders. He had brooding, dark eyes and his manner was quiet and thoughtful. I was very proud when we went out together. He talked at great length about his deep reasons for not joining the Communist Party, although he took part in the left-wing movement. I did not listen properly, it was all too complicated for me, I just gazed at him, admiring his cleverness and good looks. At the time I knew him he was estranged from his wife. I used to visit him in his flat in Soho Square. 'I am very hard-boiled!' I remember saying to him, as I draped myself on the sofa. I had seen too many B films in my schooldays. 'I think that you are very soft-boiled,' he replied in his gentle manner.

Mackendrick moved into feature films after the war, as he had told me he wanted to do. He made several well-known films such as *Mandy*, *Ladykillers* and *The Sweet Smell of Success*. Then he became Dean of the Film Department of the California Institute of Arts. According to the Film Directory, he was a subtle and individual director, whose main theme was the clash between innocence and experience. At that time there were many people in England who could not leave the country because of the war. I made many friends among the Indians. My sister Matilda had won a scholarship to Oxford University and shared a room in St Hugh's College with a pretty Indian girl with long, black, tousled hair, Parvati Kumaramangalam, who wore Indian dresses and showed us how intricately the material was wrapped around and secured with a single safety pin. On my occasional weekend visits we ate sticky sweets, which were sent to her from India, and went punting on the river. Oxford seemed so calm and peaceful with its grey towers and flowery meadows compared to wartime London. After the war Parvati returned home and eventually married the Secretary of the Indian Communist Party. Years later I met her again in Berlin when she and her husband were visiting some spa in the GDR. She was still good-looking, but stern and serious, unlike the gay young student I used to know. In London I knew several Indian writers, such as the novelist Mulk Raj Anand, the poets Tambimuttu[1] and Subramanium[2] and the then journalist Iquebal Singh. I liked these sensitive and handsome people, and became interested in the fate of India, which was at that time not independent of the British crown, and I did several drawings on the theme of the struggle for national freedom there. The Indians dispersed after the war, but I unexpectedly met Anand in Warsaw in the fifties, and again at a writer's congress in Berlin.

Iquebal Singh came to Berlin as a journalist not long after the war had ended and we had moved to Germany. I think we were living in Charlottenburg, in the British sector still, for it must have been at the time when we were friendly with the *Daily Express* correspondent

Wilfred Burchett, and I remember that we were sitting in his hotel, talking to his father, the Australian newspaperman Peter Burchett, when Iquebal came down the stairs, smiling happily, a welcome reminder of old Hampstead. Knowing that I was keenly interested in India, he had suggested that I travel to Berlin via his country, but this was not to be. He took me with him to visit the Hitler bunker, near the ruins of the Reichstag building. We went down the steps into dark and dripping concrete corridors and rooms where the macabre drama of Hitler's death had taken place. Later on it was filled in with earth and the place is as yet unmarked.

Iquebal turned up again several years later, when we were staying in a trade union holiday home, down in the Thuringian mountains. He was in a bad temper because he had been touring the GDR for two weeks as a journalist and had been obliged to live off scrambled eggs three times a day because, like many Indians, he was a vegetarian. The GDR did not seem to cater for vegetarians. In 1916 my old copy of Balzers Vegetarian Cookery lists twelve vegetarian restaurants in Berlin alone. At the moment I know of none at all in the GDR. To return to wartime London.

South Hill Park in Hampstead, London.

Paper was in short supply but there was a little left-wing monthly magazine called *Our Time*, which was devoted to cultural matters. It had a small office in Covent Garden and many of the people I knew contributed to it. It was edited by various people in turn, including the former editor of *Left Review*, Edgell Richwood. Many of the contributors to *Left Review*, which had been a larger magazine before the war, contributed to *Our Time* as its successor, though very much diminished in size. Richwood was a poet of the First World War, in which he had lost an eye in war service. He was a good editor, because he gave contributors the feeling that they could do what they liked, and he approved of it. *Our Time* published book reviews, articles on music and theatre, as well as drawings and articles on art. Frequent contributors were Randall Swingler, Arthur Calder-Marshall and Francis Klingender, the art historian who wrote *Art and the Industrial Revolution*, as well as several publications on early English caricature. I worked for *Our Time* too, sometimes doing cartoons, sometimes portraits, sometimes illustrations – much as I have always done. I did other work as well. The Communist Party passed on commissions to the Hogarth Group for art works which they needed for purpose of agitation, such as posters, leaflets etc. These jobs were mostly unpaid, but they gave me a chance to gather experience in working for the press. I carried out some small posters in the style of Mayakovski's Rosta Windows, to be put up in factories, on wall newspapers, with themes like countering anti-semitism, opening a second front in Europe and so on. I once agreed to do a large painting showing the life-and-death struggle between a heroic Russian and a Nazi for the door of Collett's bookshop in the Charing Cross Road, for which they kindly paid me five pounds, but equally kindly never put it up.

At the beginning of 1941, being twenty years old, I was called up for war service and given the choice of joining the army or working in industry. I chose industry because I had more chance of staying in London and was assigned to the post office as a lady engineer. At first I wondered if I would ever get used to the exchange, the noisy ringing of bells and the twiddly work with different coloured wires. It was not long, however, before the engineers discovered my talents, renamed me 'Rembrandt' and allowed me to the job of sign writer. I was given a battered old box of colours, with paint brushes, and told that I was centred in Willesden Exchange, but would travel round the north-west London area. I replaced two men who were called up for military service but was paid half as much as one male employee. The job had variety, and it was more interesting than having to stay in one workplace all day. In the morning at about eight, I clocked in at Willesden Exchange where I was told where to go and what should be done. I usually breakfasted first in some small café in the company of the cockroaches taking their early morning stroll. Then I went to some other exchange, or a factory, or an air base, to paint telephone numbers on switchboards, or 'This way to the air-raid shelter', or whatever else was wanted. Once I was sent to an underground bunker in Northwest London, which was designed to be a refuge for the government should the Nazis invade, and painted a telephone number beside Churchill's bed, as I was told.

8

It must have been around Christmas 1942 when a designer friend, Antony Froshaug, asked me if I would like to come with him to a party, which an artist called Graetz was giving in Hampstead. We went to the flat in number 1, South Hill Park Gardens, and found a lively medley of people sitting on the floor, strewn on the bed, chattering in various languages. René Graetz turned from one to the other, speaking French, German and English with equal ease. In the course of the evening Antony fell asleep on a bed downstairs and refused to be wakened. René accompanied me down the hill to the 24 bus stop. He said he would like to look at my studio to see if he could use it to work out a design for an exhibition. We arranged for him to come the next evening, but afterwards I remembered that I had made an appointment with Alex Mackendrick to pick me up around then. When I mentioned this to my neighbour Rowe, he said that the best thing would be for me to go to the cinema with him and forget them both, which we did, leaving the studio door open as usual. When I got back the floor was littered with Graetz's cigarette ends. He and Mackendrick had met, and the latter left first, as he told me later.

One night a rat ran out from under the bed when I came in. There was a taxidermist adjoining the studios. I went over to Rowe and spent the night there, and the next day I found a room in Charlotte Street, Soho. It was easy to find a place in those wartime days. It was above a small Italian restaurant, and soon, when I returned from work, I got used to seeing René Graetz there, eating spaghetti and nodding and smiling through the window as he waited for me. On my birthday in 1943 he came with a huge bunch of flowers and announced that he was going to rescue me from the gutter. I should move to him in Hampstead at once and he started packing my bags. His determined charm overcame me, and I moved. I was a little perturbed to see the trunks of his former girlfriend on the landing. She was going to pick them up, he assured me lightly.

9

When I think of René now, I think of his lively temperament, his charm and generosity, but above all, of the many conflicts in which he was involved, and which were an integral part of him.

His story began in Geneva, when the printer Gustav Emil Graetz married pretty, lively Elise Nebbia, whose parents were Italian immigrants. Her sister, our Tante Esther, told me that the bride, dressed in white, stood at the church door and wept. She came from a Catholic family, and after many arguments the atheist Graetz had agreed to a church wedding, but now he announced that he had changed his mind. They were married in a registry office. As you can imagine, it did not turn out to be a very harmonious marriage.

René Graetz, 1946.

Gustav Emil was of German origin and came from Polish-Russian regions from which he moved to Switzerland after the upheavals of 1905.[1] After the First World War, these regions became Polish, and he was given a Nansen pass for stateless persons. He was a social democrat, and as an admirer of the Weimar Republic; he later took German citizenship, although he continued to live in Switzerland. The newly married pair soon went on a trip to Graetz relatives in Danzig. On the way back they stopped in Berlin, where their son, René, was born. His mother died in 1918, when he was ten years old, and his roving life began, living in small hotels in Zurich, Basel or Paris, until his father married again and settled down in Geneva. The Nebbia relatives took care of René when they could, but they did not get on with Gustav Emil. 'He was as cold as ice!' said Tante Esther.

René wanted to study art, but his father insisted that he should first learn to be a printer, as he himself was. He was apprenticed at fifteen, and at nineteen his father still boxed his ears when he made a mistake. In 1929 he won a competition for a job in Cape Town, South Africa, as a printer on the *Cape Times*. He was glad to get away from his domineering parent, and with his happy, open nature, which he had inherited from his mother, he soon made friends.

He earned a good salary and, in the evening, attended the Primavera Art School, run by an expert on African art called Meyerowitz[2] and his wife. René married a girl of English descent, and a daughter was born. They bought a villa on the coast and enjoyed life in this fine climate, climbing Table Mountain and travelling in the countryside with the Meyerowitzes. However, René also took part in the anti-apartheid movement as well as the anti-Nazi demonstrations of that time and was soon estranged from his wife and her conservative family. He felt too far away from the centres of art in Europe and was easily persuaded by a beautiful girlfriend, Hetta, to go to Europe together. They travelled via Geneva and Paris to London.

Not long after their arrival the Second World War began. In 1940, after the fall of France, England expected a Nazi invasion, and to combat a possible fifth column, there was a call in the newspapers to 'Intern the lot!' referring to all German nationals, regardless of their political opinions. That included René, who travelled on a German passport because of his father's nationality.

In the internment camp in Canada, he got to know the German refugees and was persuaded to return to Germany with them after the war. An American girlfriend managed to send him art materials and so he was able to paint, if not to sculpt, in the camp. Like most left-wing artists of that time he was impressed by Picasso's *Guernica*, the first directly political painting by one of the great school of Paris. In this spirit he began to do pastel paintings showing the brutality and violence of war, in the symbolic guise of a struggle between men and centaurs. These pictures were treated with some derision, not only by the Canadian guards, but by many of the German inmates, whose understanding of art was on a low level.

In spite of this, for the first time in his life René could identify himself with a group of people. He shared the shock of internment, the uncertainty of the future and the communal existence which enabled them to withstand the stress of the internment camp. He was released, but without his large symbolic paintings. René returned to London and began to work for the German Kulturbund. He had already decided to return to Germany with the emigrants when the war was over.

'Elizabeth', 1955. Lithograph by René Graetz.

10

Hampstead is not quite London, not quite England.

The 24 bus bumbles its way up the hill to the Hampstead Heath terminus. Here the air is fresher than in other parts of the city because it is higher and because the greenness of Hampstead Heath stretches for miles over undulating country with clusters of trees and occasional sheets of water – the ponds of Hampstead. From the grassy rise of Parliament Hill, where children fly their coloured kites, there is a fine view over the city, and to the north Highgate can be seen, the highest point of London. Karl Marx is buried in Highgate Cemetery, an untidy place, but the many pilgrims cannot fail to find the famous grave, because it is marked by an outsize head of Marx, an appalling piece of sculpture, which was made in the fifties by Laurence Bradshaw, a member of the Hogarth Group. Since then, a whole crop of enormous Marx heads has sprouted in other countries, presumably because they think that the Marx family wanted it that way, which is most unlikely.

Hampstead has harboured many a refugee, and here it was that those who had fled from the Nazis founded the Free German League of Culture. It was centred in a Victorian house in Upper Park Road. When René returned from internment in Canada, he accepted a job there, designing exhibitions, posters and brochures for a small weekly wage. Among the exhibitions he designed was one called 'Allies inside Germany', which was shown in several parts of England, publicizing the activities of the German anti-Nazi movement.

Through this work, René came into contact with a cousin of Bertrand Russell, Margaret Lloyd, who was an untiring worker for different refugee causes. She had been very active in the Czech Trust Fund, an organization which helped German refugees to flee from Prague after it was occupied by the Nazis. Through Margaret, René was drawn into publicity work for the Yugoslav Emergency Committee, which promoted the cause of Tito's partisans. We were invited to a parliamentary reception to welcome the first Yugoslav partisans to visit England and shook the limp hand of the Liberal Lady Violet Bonham Carter at the entrance. Representatives of the Soviet Union were present, army officers, and I noted that they behaved with some reserve towards the partisans. Probably the rift between Moscow and Belgrade had already begun.

I only went occasionally to the Kulturbund Klub in Upper Park Road. It was very much little Germany. There was a small theatre, which showed short plays, cabaret and concerts. For these John Heartfield and Oskar Kokoschka, among others, designed the sets. This club furthered contact between the refugees and prepared for their return to their country after the war. German was spoken, weighty discussions took place, and weighty German food was eaten in the restaurant, beginning with a hearty soup. The German appetite is greater than the British, and I have heard some say that they were half-starved in England.

René and I often ate in a little Italian café near the bus terminus, where there was a modest three-course lunch for only one shilling and sixpence, and there we sometimes met Heinz Kamnitzer, a bright and lively young German historian, who had been in England quite a few years and spoke fluent, cultivated English. There were others among the refugees who hardly spoke English at all, including the president of the Kulturbund, Hans Fladung. He was a former member of the Reichstag, who had been badly beaten up by the Nazis and left for dead until he was found by the Quakers and taken to England. He was half-blind, half-deaf and walked with a stick through the streets, not really living in England, but in a dream, obsessed with plans for Germany after the war, as were all the political refugees.

Hampstead does not only harbour refugees. It is a suburb of the thoughtful, of writers and painters. We knew many of the poets – William Empson, to whom René's South African friend Hetta was married, Dylan Thomas, David Holbrook and Anna Wickham, who never washed and wore an old blue hat pulled down over her wicked old eyes. She used to tell us that she was a depressive and would hang herself one day, which she did.

In one of the old houses in Pond Street lived our friend the painter Richard Carline. The Carlines were a family of artists. The walls were covered with paintings by several generations. His mother, Anne Carline, was still alive when we first went there, her delicate naive pictures hanging among those of George, Sydney, Richard, Nancy and Hilda. Hilda had married the painter Stanley Spencer, and sometimes he was there too, small, and scruffy, with untidy hair, his jacket pockets bulging with papers, but mostly Hilda sat sadly alone by the fireside. Artists and writers came and went in this polite and kindly house. We played croquet in the beautiful sloping garden at the back of the building, followed by tea in the drawing room, among the paintings and the old-fashioned furniture, a wood fire crackling in the open grate.

The Carlines had a chest of old clothes in the corridor, long velvet dresses, shepherds' smocks, perhaps the requisites of an artist's nineteenth-century studio, maybe belonging to Dick's father and mother who were born in the 1850s, and at Christmas, led by our neighbour, May Lawrence, we would rummage in it to find a costume for the Phillips party, Dick protesting feebly and vainly. Godfrey Phillips was an art dealer who held a big party in Hampstead every year, an event originally initiated by Cliff Rowe. Dorothy Phillips, once a model for the sculptor Epstein,[1] stood with her husband at the door to greet the many guests. Very tiny, with a fine Jewish profile, she always wore a clown's costume and a friendly smile for all. Godfrey stood beside her, dressed in a Chinese silk suit with embroidered jacket. There were always two cooked turkeys on the buffet table, a sensation at this time. Later, their son told me, they had to stop giving these parties because they got out of hand. 'Strangers', he said, 'rushed in, grabbed a turkey and disappeared.'

Our before-mentioned neighbour, May Lawrence, an attractive Scottish girl, lived opposite us. She shared her flat with a succession of handsome men, finally married Ian Henderson and moved to the country after the war. Ian's mother, Wyn Henderson, had a cottage in Essex, where we sometimes went for the weekend. It was not far from London, but there was no electricity, only oil lamps and candlelight. I noted later that the electricity network seemed to be more widespread in Germany than in England at this time. At Wyn Henderson's I tasted Camembert cheese for the first time. The wartime diet was adequate, but not very varied.

Next door to us lived Richard Bennett, then editor of the monthly *Lilliput*. Not far away were the art historians Francis Klingender and Millicent Rose, with whom we were very friendly. Once Francis organized an exhibition of Russian and English caricature during the Napoleonic wars – one of his favourite subjects. It was in the AIA centre in Charlotte Street, and just as he was about to address the audience, in walked a slender, pink-and-white old man with a white beard and took a seat. Francis gulped, but managed to continue: however, no one was listening for our gaze was riveted on this fantastic figure, George Bernard Shaw himself.

Shortly before we left for Germany, the artist Paul Hogarth moved into a flat in May's house. Our acquaintance turned into a durable friendship. He was one of the few who visited us several times in Berlin. This gifted draughtsman made some of the best drawings I know of Ireland, of Belfast in particular, when he accompanied the writer Brendan Behan on a trip over there in the fifties. He co-operated with many well-known writers in reportage all over the world, with a keen eye and skilled hand.

It was nice in Hampstead. A pleasant springboard for great ventures, and a nice place to come back to. We married in Hampstead Town Hall in 1944. The day the war in Europe ended, we joined the jubilant crowds on Parliament Hill, where René sang the Marseillaise and was embraced and tossed in the air by those who thought he was a Free Frenchman. He liked that.

The German emigrants now waited impatiently for visas to allow them to return to Germany. It took some time. We went on holiday in Wales and paid a visit to Ireland.

Then at last we received Soviet visas for Berlin.

III

I

Jeder, der noch Zugang zu solchen Zeugnissen hat,
sollte sie unbedingt sichern,
denn die Zeit,
von der hier die Rede ist,
war alles andere als eine gewöhnliche.

[Anyone who still has access to such testimonies
should definitely secure them,
because the time
we are talking about
was anything but ordinary.]

From 'Die Stunde Null?' [The Zero Hour?] by Karl Max Kober, in Bildende Kunst, *Heft* 11, 1987

The refugees who wanted to return to Germany had to have an entrance visa from one of the four occupying powers, as the country was under military administration. The Russians gave entry visas first, mainly to communist refugees. The first batch went in September 1946. We went with the second group in October. Beforehand we had to undergo a series of inoculations against typhoid, cholera and so on, and hearty farewell slaps on the arm were not kindly received. Friends who had left earlier wrote to say that they had found accommodation for us – and bring candles, they urged![1] We were to live in the same house in Charlottenburg, in the British sector. They had been our neighbours in Hampstead, and we shared their joy at the end of the war, when she received news that her father, who had been arrested as a communist functionary in 1933, had been released in 1944 and married her best friend. We bought a number of cheap black tin trunks to pack our books, candles, garlic and other things, and there were several farewell parties before we set off by train, via Brussels, for Berlin. We travelled in company with Miriam, half-Jewish, returning to her divorced mother in Berlin, and two men whose names I have forgotten. One returned to England fairly soon afterwards to rejoin his wife and child who wanted to stay there.

When we approached Brussels, we were dazzled by the bright lights of peace. England was still dark and rationed, but Belgium had uranium, and flourished economically. Miriam nipped out of the train to buy a chicken for her mother, and managed it in time, while the train stood in the station. When we reached the border of the Soviet Zone, we hung out of the window to see the first Russians. I had seen one Russian officer already, walking down Piccadilly, and he was continually stopped by people who wanted to shake his hand, for in those days the Russians were looked on as heroes who had defeated the Nazi common enemy, and the tremendous sacrifices they had made, were appreciated in England too. Russians, one imagined, were over life-size, bearing golden sheaves of corn, as portrayed in the magazine *Russia Today*. We spread copies of *New Times* and red scarves around the seats, but the little soldiers who checked our passports did not seem to notice. They wore long, dirty overcoats, belted at the waist and frayed at the hem. They carried rifles, did not smile at us and looked as if they were a long way from home. It was getting dark as the train moved on to Berlin. 'What do you see?' we asked one of our companions, who was peering out at the railway lines, 'An awful lot of paper!' he replied. The train line ended at Charlottenburg. The main line stations were not yet repaired. We went down the platform to where our friends were waiting. They looked tense and drawn in the dim light.

Shadowy figures on the steps from the platform darted out, asking for cigarettes. 'Don't give them any!' muttered our companions. I had a feeling of unease, which increased when I asked how her father was. 'I'll tell you later,' she said, looking away.

It turned out that after the war ended, Soviet soldiers had come to the house and taken her father away and he had not been heard of since. One did not need to be long acquainted with the country to know that anyone released from prison in 1944 could only have agreed to serve as a decoy for the Nazis, we were told.

Our friends had booked a furnished room for us in the house where they lived. It was in the flat of a worker at the Siemens factory. Frau Baaske's husband and son had gone out during the last days of the war and never returned. Their clothes hung still in the wardrobe of our room, and as Frau Baaske's hope that they were still alive faded, trousers were swapped for potatoes on the black market. Apart from the clothes cupboard, there was one filled with glasses of various sizes, and a few rolled-up carpets in the corner, presumably destined for barter too. With our nine tin trunks, piled on top of each other, an ancient couch, a table with a lacy cloth, two beds and an old-fashioned stove, there was not much room to move.

During the succeeding days, we moved the table to the window, which looked out on to a grey backyard, but where there was a little more daylight for me to draw caricatures for the press, which the comrades immediately demanded. Electric current was limited to about two hours a day, so we were glad to have those candles we had brought. Frau Baaske managed our ration cards and cooked for us, all too complicated for newcomers. At the corner of the street was the black market, where various goods were sold or bartered, interrupted occasionally by a police raid. Then the shoppers scattered, but soon returned. There were little notices pinned to the trees offering sale or exchange. I remember one which read, 'Would gladly exchange my husband for a big fat pig!' The only thing that seemed to be unrationed was salt, displayed freely in the empty shop windows.

I was told by Frau Baaske not to open the door to anyone in her absence. Beggars pleading for something to eat were constant callers. It was a long, icy winter. Snow fell in November and only melted in March. Among the terrible ruins which surrounded us, people searched for firewood. In the morning, Frau Baaske often came in with the news that this or that neighbour had hanged himself in the night.

'First impressions of Berlin, 1946'.

'First impressions of Berlin, 1946'.

The thing to do, we were told, was to find a British soldier who would be prepared to receive parcels for us, which could not apparently be sent directly. Someone put us in touch with the *Daily Express* correspondent, Wilfred Burchett, who kindly agreed to be our post office. René had made a commercial agreement with a Swiss firm, who sent us nice strawberry jam and such things. The Culture Club, an elegant building in the Jägerstraße, provided a hot meal for its cultured members who produced the necessary ticket. Only one ticket per family was issued, and this was of course given to the men, which made me slightly indignant, but René kindly allowed me to use his occasionally. One day Frau Baaske invited us to join her in a visit to the opera in Admiralspalast, later Metropol-Theater, newly restored by the Russians, and in the interval, she led us, beaming, to the buffet, where we ate a saucer of beetroot, donated by the Russians – and unrationed!

It was a strange small world we had joined. For the outsider, the Germans were divided into two categories: the Nazis, the Nazi army and their supporters – the guilty ones – and the anti-Nazis, who had emerged from camps and prisons, or returned from emigration abroad. The image of the first category was for me strongly influenced by the caricatures in wartime publications: the German with shaved head, sharp nose and spectacles, obedient and slavish. The main political directive given to those who returned to Germany was that the Germans should realize that they had been responsible for the outbreak of this terrible war, that they should admit their German guilt.

René began right away to discuss this question with our landlady and her boyfriend as they sat together in the kitchen one evening. 'Yes,' said the boyfriend thoughtfully, after an impassioned speech by René, 'we made a mistake. We should have invaded England.' The second category of Germans were the tested opponents of regime. The military government distributed jobs to them, often more on grounds of political reliability than professional qualifications.

'Berlin Sketches, 1946: Smokers' Area'. *Berlin am Mittag* (10.2.47).

During that first autumn we were very busy. René was trying to continue the work he had done in England, making portable exhibitions on art education, using material he had brought. He was employed by the main educational publishing house, but it was difficult to make any headway. Modern art, even the French Impressionists, were frowned on as formalist, as indeed was every other school of contemporary painting and sculpture except the naturalistic Soviet style. There was, however, an eager interest in modern art among the general public, and I remember seeing a long queue for an exhibition of modern French painting, never shown during the Nazi rule, in the part of the Schloss which was still standing in Unter den Linden.

René went off in the morning to work in the educational publishing house. My workplace was our furnished room, where I turned out drawings for the papers. We came into contact with artists at a big exhibition in Dresden in the autumn of 1946, where we met many future friends. We stayed with a sculptor and his actress wife – who both moved to the West not long afterwards – on the hill of Weißer Hirsch. Their account of the bombing and the last days of the war was horrific. Dresden was a sea of ruins. From Weißer Hirsch one looked down on a desolate landscape of scattered stones, with a few paths winding between them. We were told of the massive and persistent bombing of the city by the Allies at a time when it was known that the war was coming to an end, of the machine-gunning of the terrified citizens who had fled to the flat green banks of the River Elbe, followed by the entry of the Russian troops. Our actress friend had developed a nervous shake of the head, which increased as she told us bitterly of their past experiences and their distrust of the present. I recalled how we in England rejoiced to see fleets of planes setting out to bomb Germany because it meant that the war would soon be over. So callous, so insensitive are we made by war.

The Russians invited the artists to a banquet in their headquarters on the hill, one of a number of grand villas in spacious grounds, which had been spared the bombing. I noted that our hosts looked at me coldly when we were introduced as having just arrived from England. As I could not yet converse in German, I was placed next to the painter Schmidt-Rottluff,[2] who spoke French. Neither of us spoke French very well, and no remarks were passed worth recording. I wish I had known then that I was sitting with one of the famous founders of Expressionism. At a reception given by the British cultural attaché in Charlottenburg we again met several artists and writers. There I first met Herbert Sandberg. He visited us shortly afterwards with his pretty wife and they sat with us by candlelight on Frau Baaske's old sofa, and exuded optimism. He had been released from Buchenwald concentration camp not long before, after eleven years imprisonment. He was effervescent with vitality and a desire to make up for the long years of frustration. He was not only a caricaturist but editor of the satirical magazine *Ulenspiegel* for which he asked me to work. *Ulenspiegel* was in the tradition of *Simplicissimus*, which I had known and admired in England long before. It existed only a few years, until the final division of Germany, but during this time it achieved a reputation with a wide range of contributors as a fresh, spirited and intelligent publication, from East and West. At this reception we met two young men who bowed and kissed my hand very politely, and René whispered that they were Wolfgang Harich and Wolfgang Leonard, the most promising of the young intellectuals. It was difficult for someone coming from abroad to imagine life under Nazi rule, the brutality to which people had been subjected, their doubt and impotence as to the possibility of resistance, the horrors of war and the shock of defeat, but it was all written on the faces in the street. Germany had reached the bottom of an abyss. There was a kind of vacuum. Any optimism was greeted with eagerness, new life was springing out of the ruins, everything seemed possible, everyone was needed.

2

When we first arrived in Berlin, René went to the authorities to register our presence and received the first box on the ear from his fatherland. He was told he was not a German but stateless, because he had never lived in Germany. He felt a little rejected at first, but it turned out to be an advantage for him at that time because being stateless was like being a foreigner as far as travel was concerned. Under military administration, Germans were subject to certain travel restrictions and it was difficult to move in and out of the country. At the end of 1946 we were able to go to Paris for the foundation of UNESCO, and to see the international art exhibition, in which René had a large painting of centaurs, done during his internment in Canada. It was hung in the section for displaced persons, as the Germans were not represented.

René picked me up from hospital in Spandau, where I had been in for a miscarriage, and we went straight to the station. We travelled by train in the foreigners' compartment, which meant that we did not have to get out at stations to be checked, as the Germans did. We did not have seats however, and I lay on the floor on the corridor with a British army officer, just out of hospital too, with a plaster cast on his leg. Travelling through the

Ruhr, we saw that life in the industrial West of Germany was then harder than in the East after the destruction of war. We passed what were known as 'Potato Trains', full of people heading for the countryside to barter their possessions for food. They clung to the outside of the carriages, and sat on the roof, clutching sacks of goods to be exchanged. When we got to Paris, a city without ruins, and began to search for our hotel in Montparnasse, I developed a haemorrhage, the luggage was heavy, and we were tired. But then we found the hotel, there was our friend Dick Carline, and although I had to stay in bed for a few days, everything was wonderful. Post-war life in France was not easy either. The cafés served only a little plate of carrots unrationed, and – great hardship for the French – they were only allowed one bottle of wine a week. This the customers labelled and left on the shelf of their usual café for the occasional sip. There was of course a black market for those who could afford it.

We celebrated New Year at Neuilly with an artist acquaintance of Carline's, a White Russian[1] called Prince Ivanov. We could not find the address at first and as it was nearing midnight, we dropped into a police station to ask for help. It turned out that Prince Ivanovs were legion in Paris, but finally we found the one we were seeking, and the coronets embroidered on the cushion covers emphasized his claim to aristocracy. He and Madame de Troudon would have been well met in the Bois de Boulogne. I paid a brief visit to London for a few days to see friends, and the editor of *Lilliput*, for which I had worked, suggested that I might be appointed foreign correspondent of the magazine, to improve our material conditions, and we went together to the War Office in Whitehall to apply, but they turned me down.

Then I returned to Paris, where we spent a few more days. We went several times to the large international art exhibition, where René's centaur painting was hanging. This picture was scorned by the East German art critics, but much later it was bought by the National Gallery, when the anti-formalist campaign was dropped. This picture was shown, as already mentioned, in the department for stateless artists. Then the hatred and anger against the Germans was very evident. Once I ventured to remark to someone that life was hard in Germany too at that time, but she turned away in rage, retorting, 'I don't want to hear about it! As far as I am concerned, they can all go to hell!'

It was the time of the existentialists – Sartre and Simone de Beauvoir. We went to see Sartre's *Huis Clos* in a little theatre. It is about a vision of hell, that being people who are eternally locked into one room. That, and the close, airless atmosphere, induced one woman to faint, and she had to be carried out, and I felt a rising panic and was vastly relieved when the play was over.

After we returned to the grim ruins of Berlin, we moved into a large empty room in Zehlendorf, in the American sector. It was in a suburb called Onkel Toms Hütte [Uncle Tom's Cabin], and the small house had been built by a well-known modern architect called Taut.[2] We shared it with our friend Miriam and her husband, the actor Gerry Wolf. We lived on the first floor, Wolf upstairs, and we shared kitchen and bath down below. The surroundings were greener and there was room to work. René gave up his job at *Volk und Wissen* and began to work as a freelance artist.

'Berlin Sketches, 1946: Hats'. *Berlin am Mittag* (08.02.1947).

We were friendly then with Georg Honigmann and his wife, Litzi. He had worked as a foreign correspondent for Reuters in England and was now editor of a new paper called *BAM* (*Berlin am Mittag*), for which he asked me to work. Among other commissions, I got the nice job of attending first nights of all the theatres in Berlin, to make caricatures of the actors. Being sort of deaf and dumb, I did not profit so much as I might have done, but I saw the legendary Gustav Gründgens in his production of *The Shadow*, by Jewgeni Schwarz, before he moved to Hamburg. The impression of this piece in the Deutsches Theater has always remained in my memory as a picture of the strange unreal atmosphere of Berlin at this time, the political tension and almost nightmarish uncertainty about the future.

'Berlin Sketches, 1946: Politeness Week'. *Berlin am Mittag*, (22.02.1947).

We needed some furniture in our large empty room in Onkel Toms Hütte, and Georg gave us a sort of couch from the *BAM* office. It had an aluminium framework and three orange cushions, and we thought it was very smart. We had some adjustable furniture made, which cost a fortune; it consisted of four pieces which could be pushed together or taken apart and resembled the furniture we had seen in the flat where we had stayed in Dresden. So now we were furnished and felt more settled in our new quarters.

3

While we were living in Zehlendorf, René came home one day in a state of great excitement. Breathlessly he announced that there was a search on for thieves who had stolen paintings from the famous Dresden collection, during the chaos at the end of the war, and it had been discovered that they planned to cut Raphael's *Mother and Child* into four pieces to be sold abroad, and this must be prevented – we must help, both of us! How much of all this was true, I do not know, but René loved art as I have never known anyone else to do, and it was no problem to win him for such an undertaking. An ancient white American coupé picked us up next day driven by a plain-clothes policeman, who showed us his revolver, to inspire confidence I suppose. We drove to Dresden, where we were given instructions as to what we should do. We should meet the thief at the appointed house and pretend to be Americans who wanted to buy pictures. We went there with the man who had made the appointment. A bottle of rum stood on the table as one of the props, and René, very excited, took a good gulp of it. The thief arrived with a suitcase of pictures, and before he barely had time to take them out, the policeman opened the window, a signal for those outside to come in, and so they did, storming the house with revolvers at the ready, and cries of 'Hands up!' René, still in his role as an accomplice, threw himself on the startled officers. 'You are much too early!' he hissed at them, 'I was just going to find out where more pictures are hidden! Arrest her!' He pointed to me, and the bewildered policeman nervously took hold of my wrist. I had to laugh, I could not help it, although I felt sorry for the poor thief, who had turned very pale. 'I thought,' said René afterwards, 'that when we all sat together in prison, he would tell me more!' But our part in the melodrama was over, and we were told we could return home.

4

Hush-a-bye baby on the tree-top,
When the wind blows the cradle will rock;
When the bough breaks the cradle will fall
Down comes the baby cradle and all!

English lullaby

In the autumn of 1947 I discovered that I was pregnant. I decided to go to England and stay with my mother until the baby was born because the diet was better – free orange juice and cod liver oil had produced a generation of strapping babies – and I could buy all the necessary equipment. After several mishaps I was very happy to be pregnant and anxious that all should go well.

René and I travelled together to sleepy Bedford. Not long after we arrived my father was taken very ill and the day after René left to return to Berlin, he died. I was glad we had been there during this difficult time for my mother.

I was booked in at Bedford County Hospital, which specialized in complicated births. My daughter Anne arrived prematurely in the early morning of the second of January – just missing New Year's Day but raising a groan in succeeding years because of this birthday just when one was recovering from seasonal festivities and the shops were shut for stocktaking.

She was very tiny, with a great deal of soft brown hair on her head and back, and her fingernails were not fully grown. She was not quite ready for the world and was always fast asleep when she was brought to me. Once, after the nurses had put salt on her tongue and pinched her poor little toes so that she would wake up and feed, she opened her violet eyes, looked out and said 'Oh!' Then she closed them again and went back to sleep.

We were in a large ward with two long rows of beds, facing each other in old-style fashion. I am in favour of such wards, provided they have curtains between the beds, which can be drawn if one wants privacy. In a big ward one can see what the staff are doing, and the many patients provide diversion. In rooms with two or three beds, one feels obliged to keep up conversation with the fellow patients, and one suspects the nurses of drinking coffee in their recreation room all day.

Elizabeth, Matilda Clegg and René Graetz in Lyme Regis, England, 1948.

In the ward where my baby was born, there were two other women whose husbands were absent. One was a poor orphan whose granny had thrown her out and she had been taken in by a home for expectant mothers on condition that her baby should be offered for adoption at birth. She was in hospital already because of high blood pressure, no wonder. The other was a fairly tough prostitute, who was brought in one evening, straight from the pub, where the birth had already begun. A very tiny, premature infant was born shortly afterwards and put in a glass incubator, where it lay naked except for a frilly bonnet askew on its head. It had enormous vitality, and loud yells were uttered from its large mouth, except when milk was poured in, direct to its stomach through a rubber tube. The mother of this child and I were not allowed to have our babies in the ward at visiting time because of the risk of infection, so we sat together and chatted, while I marvelled at the slow growth of a maternal instinct in my companion. I fear however that it did not last.

I was crazy about my baby. When we were allowed home, she still had to be fed every three hours day and night, and as each feed took an hour, this was a full-time occupation for some weeks. I read books about diets and babies, and when my mother went to Ireland for a couple of months to stay with her family, I went to my sister in Oxford, who already had two babies, and we talked about babies, babies, until one day I suddenly remembered that I could draw, and felt a great surge of joy and lightness as I realized that I was getting bored with all this exclusive baby talk and needed to return to normal life. I went to London and stayed with May Henderson in Hampstead, and as we sat dandling our babies on our knees, David Holbrook dropped past and said, 'I wonder what you two would have said if you could have seen yourselves as you are now, a year ago?' 'We'd have jumped straight out of the window, I expect!' said May cheerfully.

I had sent my passport to London for renewal and the necessary visa for Berlin but had no reply until I heard that it had been mislaid. Then I was told to come for an interview at the Foreign Office, where I was treated with some hostility, but given a visa for Berlin. I was informed that as I was married to a German, it was possible for me to acquire double nationality, but that they did not like it. René came over to fetch me back, looking thin and nervy. With my mother, my sister and her family and my good baby who never cried, we went on holiday to Lyme Regis and then returned to Berlin by plane. The Cold War was intensifying rapidly. The blockade of West Berlin had begun, and we hoped that we would not be 'buzzed' by Russian Migs.

René Graetz and daughter Anne in Zehlendorf, Berlin, 1949.

Then separate East–West currencies were introduced, and two separate states were formed. We moved over the border to the Soviet Zone, where the money we earned was valid. René applied in October 1949 for citizenship of the newly founded German Democratic Republic. He went to the police to pick up his identity card and came back with one for me as well. 'They gave me this for you,' he said. I remembered that the British Foreign Office disapproved, but I thought it of little consequence. When I married René in 1944, I lost my British nationality and became a Friendly Enemy Alien, as the law then was. I recovered my British citizenship later in a magistrate's court and was then listed as a naturalized British subject. The law that women lost their nationality on marriage with a foreigner was eventually revoked.

In old German law, women automatically became German when they married a German, but in 1948 this clause was changed, and women should make an application themselves for German citizenship in the interest of equality. I did not know this at the time but decades later, when a new law on citizenship was published, I was able, after some negotiation, to discard my GDR nationality, on the grounds that I had never applied for it. That enabled me to travel more freely. Now, however, the Cold War had begun, and the door clanged shut for six years, during which I was given no exit visa to leave the country, and to ensure this I had to give up my British passport into safe-keeping. In my own interest, I was assured. A restriction on travel lasting six years may not seem much to the generations in the GDR who have grown up since 1961. The demand for the right to travel freely which is so widespread today is not because people yearn to pile into jumbo jets and take part in that crazy phenomenon known as modern tourism, but because they resent not being able to decide themselves where and when they want to go, on pleasure or business. This kind of tutelage is an insult, and so I felt it too, especially as I had settled in the country of my own free will.

'The Distance Exchange East, and the Distance Exchange West', *Ulenspiegel*, 1948.

5

Die Partei, die Partei, die hat immer recht
Die Partei, die Partei, die Partei …
[The Party, the Party, is always right,
the Party, the Party, the Party …]

Verse by Louis Fürnberg
Music by Ernst Hermann Meyer

On 2 January 1949, we moved from Onkel Toms Hütte in the American Sector to Kleinmachnow in the Soviet Zone, just beyond the Berlin border. The musician Ernst Hermann Meyer and his English wife, Marjorie, lived there and introduced us to the musicologist Nathan Notowicz and his Dutch wife, Ann. They had just arrived from Holland, and we decided to share a house with several rooms, kitchen and bathroom in common.

Most of our acquaintances had moved from West Berlin to Kleinmachnow because the trip through West Berlin to the centre of town was then easy, but as the hostility between East and West increased, the connection became more difficult. From time to time the border was closed, and so the long tiresome journey round the borders of Berlin was necessary. That meant that we became more dependent on each other for social life, and at weekends we used to meet together at this or the other house.

Picnic in Kleinmachnow, 1950. Photograph by Priscilla Siebert. From left to right: Elizabeth, René Graetz, Nathan Notowicz, Majorie Meyer, Hans Siebert, Ernst H. Meyer, Josef Winternitz.

One of our most prominent neighbours was Robert Havemann. He lived in a comfortable house, a few doors away from us, not long before he had been freed from the death cell of the Nazi prison in Brandenburg. It was difficult to imagine that this tall, lively man with his shining, smiling face, had been through such a terrible experience. He was a friendly person and often gave us a lift into the city in his car – cars were rare in those days. When he saw my high English pram he was fascinated, and we arranged an exchange whereby I swapped it for the Havemann pram, easier to manage on public transport. Robert was then a highly respected citizen, Professor of Physics, Member of Parliament, much photographed in demonstrations for peace in West Berlin. He was the first of our circle to be invited to Moscow and we listened excitedly as he retailed anecdotes of his trip. Later, like most of us, the Havemanns moved back into Berlin. He invited us to visit his flat in Strausberger Platz, where a picture of a pipe-smoking Stalin hung on the wall.

Elizabeth Shaw and daughter Anne in Kleinmachnow, 1949.

'Why don't you take down that picture?' we protested, after Khrushchev's revelations at the twentieth Party Congress. Havemann smiled secretively, did not answer, but turned up the music of his tape recorder. He had the habit of keeping a finger on this machine during conversations: he talked, and before anyone else could answer loud music intervened. It was Havemann's strength, but also his weakness, that he could not listen to any opinion but his own. In the years that followed he developed the concept of democratic socialism, and gave a course of lectures on the subject in the Humboldt University, an undertaking which earned him the rage and hatred of the party apparatus. He was expelled from the party, from the Academy of Science, stripped of all honours and public posts, and so he retired to his *Datscha* in the village of Grünheide.

'It doesn't matter,' he said, when we first visited him there, 'I have saved up enough money. I can live without any income for a few years.'

He, who was always so generous when others needed money, had to hold out for a long time. He was not imprisoned. A more gruesome fate awaited him. His abode was placed under police surveillance. His circle of young admirers was followed, questioned, persecuted. He was forced into isolation. This robust man took on a haggard look and a melancholy, wounded expression grew on his face.

In the documentary film *1945* by Karl Gass, the death cell in Brandenburg Prison is shown, and as the camera moves over the wall, the name 'B. Havemann' is to be seen, scratched on the stone. He was a dreamer of the realistic variety, and I think, or would like to think, that he foresaw the later development of a liberal democratic socialism.

But to return to Kleinmachnow in 1949. Opposite us lived the caricaturist Herbert Sandberg, who had been released from Buchenwald concentration camp four years previously. A little further down the road lived an artist colleague from London, Priscilla Siebert, with her husband and two small children. Our international circle was enriched by Musy Henschel, who was married to the son of the publisher Henschel. When she arrived from Paris, and, leaning on the Notowicz piano, sang 'Sous les toits de Paris …', René was in seventh heaven and I was jealous of this blonde singer, who later became a dear friend.

Elizabeth Shaw and Herbert Sandberg during the 1 May Marches, 1951.

We women shared the task of shopping and caring for the children in an easy fashion together. When Ann's second child was born, like a good Dutch woman she rode off to the hospital on a bicycle, her husband cycling watchfully behind her. My son, who was named Patrick to remind him of his forebears, was born a year later. Musy had fixed up with her doctor that I could come to the Charité and when my son announced his impending arrival rather unexpectedly, we rattled off in a milk van, which probably accelerated the birth, which took place speedily though feet first, just after we got to the hospital.

We were all great admirers of Stalin and convinced that only good could come from Moscow – even though it was sometimes puzzling. The Rajk trial in Hungary shocked us – how could faithful old comrades suddenly become such traitors? Our artist friend from London came by one day to tell us that her brother-in-law, Field, was an American spy (later rehabilitated). He was in prison, so her husband had lost his job and they had to move to Dresden. In their own interest, it was emphasized. Most of us took part in Marxist educational courses, either through night classes, or a course which was called the Stalin Biography. Even René, who was continually under attack as a formalist artist, was convinced that the party, to which he had dedicated himself, could make no mistake.

In the evening, after the children were in bed, it was wonderfully quiet, and René and I worked together in our large living room, often until the early hours of the morning. He tried obediently to paint in the style of so-called socialist realism, painted again and again a picture of a meeting in a factory, which never improved. I was busy with my drawings for *Ulenspiegel* and for the daily newspapers. Sometimes a Notowicz dropped in, to borrow a cigarette or have a chat. It was a sociable time. Once, I went to the Meyers to have a bath. They were the only ones to possess this luxury, and kindly allowed others to share it. When I came in, I found Ernst sitting at the piano composing, while the poet Louis Fürnberg, wearing his hearing aid, walked up and down and sang:

'Die Partei, die Partei, die hat immer Recht,
Die Partei, die Partei, die Partei ...'
That is the way we were.

Ulenspiegel, 1949: 'Congratulations, Mother Germania, Triplets.'[1]

6

In 1949 René worked with enthusiasm on a project for a large mural in Dresden, and later on a second mural in the mining town of Ballenstedt. He was part of a collective, consisting of three other painters: Strempel, Mohr and Bruse.[1] Thin, bearded Horst Strempel led the team. They intended to carry out a wall painting in the Mexican tradition.

However, their work was harshly attacked in the newspaper as formalist, and there were brutal confrontations with the functionaries of that time. One of the results was that Strempel, old anti-Nazi, taking his bedding on his shoulder, left by night with wife and child for West Berlin. It was a leap, however, from frying pan into the fire, for in the western part of the city there was a dictatorship of the abstract artists, and they wanted no part of him. It was a terrible time and left deep scars on René. Even in his last years he would wake at night and tell me of nightmares about the quarrels of those days with people whose names I had long forgotten. He was strangely affected by the attacks on him, so that he began to wonder if critics were not right – after all, they were politically proved Marxists. He began to paint in a style which might be acceptable, works which he later destroyed. Then he returned to sculpture. He worked for a time on a Thälmann[2] monument, but left it as he disagreed with the conception, then made a statue of the Greek partisan hero Belojannis and was part of the collective which erected a monument commemorating the sufferings of Buchenwald concentration camp.

René found a sculptor's studio in Pankow, the Soviet sector of Berlin, and a flat not far away. We had to get something called a 'Zuzug' to move back into Berlin, and this was not at all easy. It was like waiting for the visa in London. Our flat was in the Kavalierstraße. It seemed dark and narrow to me – four flights of gloomy stairs, and no garden for the children. I missed the camaraderie of our neighbours in Kleinmachnow, particularly the women, and our social life seemed to consist mostly of visits to Horst Strempel, or to Mart Stam from Holland, who was currently working at the art school, and both complained bitterly and endlessly of their disillusion about the state of art and society in socialism, compared to their hopes during the Weimar Republic.

Then the children were often sick. They had whooping cough and on top of it measles, and before that was over, my son developed scarlet fever and was put in hospital, where he got chickenpox. In the meantime, my daughter, who had been sent on holiday with her kindergarten, came home with suspected dysentery and had to go to hospital too. I was working as a cartoonist for *Neues Deutschland* then, and when I was told that I could fetch both children from hospital, I rang up the editorial department and told them that I was going to take time off to concentrate on my family. So we went for walks in the park, and I coddled them properly so that I was only half aware that there was an escalating crisis over norms in industry, which culminated in the riots of 17 June 1953. When the tumult began, I had gone for a walk in the park with the children as usual, and coming back, I met our concierge on the street in front of the house. She stopped me to say that there were long queues at the grocer and people were buying everything up. Was there going to be a war? Then René approached, bearing twelve tins of Russian crab. He said he could not get anything else, and as everyone seemed to be shopping in panic, he thought he should take something along. Now he had been told to report at the local party headquarters and must be off! I went upstairs and turned on the radio. The Soviet Military Command of Berlin announced that they had taken over the administration of the city and that martial law would be in force from midday onwards. This announcement was repeated at intervals, with sonorous music in between. I felt that I should do something, so I rang up the editorial department of *Neues Deutschland* and asked if I was needed. I was greeted with hysterical laughter and the question as to how it was in my locality. As I heard later, in the centre of the city a throng of demonstrators surged through the streets. They were mainly from the factories, where their dissatisfaction with the economic and political situation had reached boiling point and they demanded radical charges. Hundreds had been leaving for the West in the previous months, and it was clear that the situation could not continue.

Towards the evening René had not yet returned, and a neighbour rang up to say that her husband was away on duty too and she would like to come round, because she was afraid. She was an old, experienced anti-Nazi, and I was surprised to hear that she was afraid. As we sat together, we heard the heavy rattle of Soviet tanks moving down to take up position in the Schlosspark at the end of the street, where there were government offices in the one-time palace. 'Thank goodness,' said the old comrade, 'that we have the Soviet tanks near us!'

René came home before nine, because during martial law no one was allowed on the street after that. He had been bravely arguing with dissatisfied citizens about the state of affairs, but with little success, he said. The Soviet tanks remained in the park for some days. The park keeper walked up and down in a rage, waving his stick, and complaining about what they were doing to the grass. Although I did not experience much of the riots of 17 June in Berlin, these events had an effect on me in the long term. I could no longer naively assume that the majority of the population supported the government. In succeeding days, high functionaries were to be seen wandering round the local grocery store, looking to see what was offered for sale, listening to what people said. They had to get in touch with reality.

I too, had to come down to earth with a jolt.

7

I had now been working as a political caricaturist for over ten years. It had been especially rewarding when I worked for Sandberg's *Ulenspiegel*, with its merry discussions at editorial meetings, and the possibility of using colour. However, in 1949 the licence for the magazine was taken away – it was a victim of the Cold War. Shortly afterwards I was invited to have a talk with Rudolf Herrnstadt, the chief editor of the party paper *Neues Deutschland*, who offered me a job as caricaturist with a regular fixed sum, paid monthly, very welcome to a family where one member was in disgrace for being a formalist. I was happy too to work with such an excellent journalist as Herrnstadt, who was already famous for an article called 'We and the Russians' dealing frankly with relations between the Germans and the Soviet occupation.

Eulenspiegel, 1950s: 'Adenauer: The Paris Agreements Secure Germany's Future.'[1]

I was given a room in the editorial building, and attended the editorial morning meetings, presided over by Herrnstadt. After that I discussed the caricature relevant to the topic of the day with a young member of the editorial team, Arne Rehahn, with whom I enjoyed working too. I liked the challenge of being allowed a theme, analysing it, and condensing it to a particular point. I even liked the pressure of the deadline, which demanded rapid decision, and prevented one from going too deeply into the subject matter. Like an actor, I enjoyed the applause too, and I think I even believed that I was influencing the audience.

I studied the work of Vicky and Low,[2] as well as the Kukryniksys.[3] As my German was extremely faulty, my texts were constructed by others, and I spent a lot of time scratching out my spelling mistakes with a razor blade. I was not really productive or speedy enough for a daily newspaper.

After 17 June 1953 there was a crisis in upper party circles. Stalin was dead, echoes of the succeeding power struggle reached Berlin. Herrnstadt lost his seat in the Politbüro, his job as editor of the party newspaper, and with him his close collaborators on the staff, including Arne Rehahn. They were all dispersed to work in other publications or jobs of little public significance, and I had no partner any more in the editorial department with whom I could discuss my ideas for the daily cartoon. The close preoccupation with daily events that was necessary as a journalist became irksome. I could not work in colour for the daily press, and this narrowed my scope as an artist. I gradually withdrew to work freelance for various weekly and monthly magazines and as a book illustrator. This was financially a drawback for us because I no longer received a fixed sum, which had meant a certain stability in our finances, but I was able to expand artistically and it made life easier as a mother too, when I began to work at home again.

In 1954 I applied once more to the police for an exit permit to visit England, and in the new post-Stalinist political situation this was granted. I got my passport back and kept it and went with the children on a pleasant holiday, which lasted six weeks, visiting friends and relatives in Devon, Essex, Oxford and London. I had been very homesick, and it did me good. After that I went to England almost every year. I began to live with a foot in two countries: one in which I worked and to which my family belonged, the other in which I still felt ties of language and friendship.

8

'Fate chooses your relations, you choose your friends,' said the Abbé Delille a couple of hundred years ago.

For René and for me, and our children, friends were very important, not only because we were gregarious by nature, but because we had no relatives in Germany. I have always been curious about new places and people and assumed that everyone else is too, but quite late in life I have discovered that this is not the case. However, there were many others in the years just after the Second World War who had come from abroad and were glad to make contact with people in the same situation. We met them mostly in the Culture Club – Klub der Kulturschaffenden – a rather pompous building, once called the Herrenklub, the Gentlemen's Club, which offered a hamburger and two veg to members, mostly male, in hard times. There, one was introduced to people who had returned from emigration to remote places like America or Mexico, or had come out of Nazi concentration camps, and of course it was a meeting place for acquaintances from the London emigration. It was nice to be able to talk English, and it was a point of contact for professional projects, in those days before artists' unions had been founded.

Elizabeth Shaw and son Patrick in Kleinmachnow, Berlin, 1950.

There were other points of contact too, like Pinzke's bookshop. It was under the railway bridge in Friedrichstraße, where the whores used to parade up and down, sheltered from the rain. Pinzke, a small man with dark, sad, intelligent eyes, sat in the back room and received friends who dropped in when passing – and they were many – showing them bibliophile treasures he had acquired. Pinzke had been an active anti-Nazi and lived in a small villa, which had been built for the SS guards in the nearby Sachsenhausen concentration camp. In 1948, shortly after I returned from England with my baby, we were invited to a large party there, and everyone we knew seemed to be present. A year later, at the time of the Rajk show trial in Hungary, a close friend of Pinzke called Creikemeyer, who was in charge of the railways, was arrested and imprisoned; and we heard sadly that Pinzke had committed suicide. Was friendship dangerous?

Only decades later did it become clear that we and all those who had returned from western emigration were listed as enemies of the state, along with anyone who had dissident opinions, and destined for internment, imprisonment, or execution.

Illustration for Friedrich Wolf. *Tiergeschichten* [Animal Stories], 1951.

During the fifties the friendly chief editor of the Aufbau Verlag, Max Schroeder, commissioned me to illustrate a book by Mark Twain for them. Much earlier I had illustrated some stories by Friedrich Wolf at the author's request, and had visited him in his home with Alfred Holz, who published the book. After that I left book illustration to concentrate on caricature for the press, which interested me more at the time. Now, however, I began to draw mainly for the Aufbau Verlag and the monthly cultural magazine *Aufbau*, which was edited by Bodo Uhse.

We met the Uhses around 1952, when we lived in the Kavalierstraße. It was one of those black times when art and artists were in an impasse because of the discussion about formalism, and the children seemed to be so often sick. I was still missing the social life in Kleinmachnow. Bodo was married to Alma, an American, and they lived a little outside Berlin, near Potsdam, in a house on the edge of a lake. Alma kept a horse and went riding in the forest, and looked after her two boys, the elder of which was the son of the American writer James Agee, to whom she had been married before she met Bodo in Mexico.

Illustration for Mark Twain. *Humoristische Erzählungen* [Humorous Stories], 1958.

She was delightfully frank and honest but seemed strangely out of touch with life around her, and in fact never really adapted herself to living abroad. The smell of wood fire and horse reminded me of my grandmother's farm. Bodo laughed at my jokes, which caused most Germans to look at me blankly, and I felt very easy and at home.

Elizabeth Shaw. Photograph by Paul Wiens, at the World Youth Festival in Warsaw, 1955.

Bodo asked me to contribute regularly to *Aufbau*, and I often met him for lunch in town. We discussed the events of the day and there was a note of sceptical irony in his remarks which interested me. The revelations of Khrushchev about the crimes committed under Stalin affected him very deeply and threw him off balance in his work and in his private life. He found himself unable to continue the massive novel *Patriots*, which he had begun, and in the desperate search for a new stimulus he and Alma became estranged, and she returned to New York with her sons. In the mid-fifties Bodo Uhse was socially extremely active. He had functions in the Writers' Union, in PEN, in the Academy of Arts, and was a member of the Chamber of Deputies. After the Hungarian uprising he was obliged to attend the show trial of Walter Janka, director of the Aufbau publishing house, who was accused of plotting a counter-revolution. Bodo had known Janka when they were both in the International Brigade, during the Spanish Civil War, then during the emigration in Mexico, as well as in Berlin. He did not have the courage – and he was not the only one – to protest against the trial, and he became deeply depressed: the disintegration of his personality increased, he drank heavily and finally died in 1965. In 1956 there was a writers' congress in Berlin, and I was asked to make a series of caricatures of well-known writers to be put up in the entrance hall. When Bodo saw my drawings he suggested that they should be made into a brochure and we went together to Janka who agreed, and organized speedy printing of the venture. Paul Wiens was commissioned to write verses to accompany the drawings. Bodo, Wiens and I met then frequently in the press club to discuss ideas for the series, my knowledge of modern German literature being slight. I had got to know Paul in Warsaw, during the World Youth Festival of 1955. He was half-Jewish, possessed charm and wit and was very cultivated. He had grown up in England and Switzerland, where his mother had taken him, when his Nazi father divorced her. He was a young dreamer when he returned to Nazi Germany and was arrested and imprisoned with several Russians, from whom he then learned to speak fluent Russian. I liked Paul very much, and we stayed good friends until his too early death, at the age of fifty-nine.

With this brochure, my portrait phase began. In my youth I had sometimes drawn portraits of friends, with a leaning towards caricature, which was not always pleasing. I remember once a girlfriend in London, Dulcie Butterfield, asked me to draw her, and when I obliged, she looked at it, smiled politely, and then tore it into pieces, screaming, 'You little beast!' I was totally shocked, and our friendship cooled rapidly.

As a political caricaturist I had to draw portraits, but of course from photographs, which I found unsatisfactory, and when I was asked to draw the writers I always tried to make sketches from life. Drawings seem to fascinate the onlooker. Once I was just a few hours in Morocco, in Tangier, and there I sketched an old man on the harbour. He was wearing a long brown coat with a hood, which he used as a shopping bag. A loaf of bread was visible. He saw me drawing but did not seem to mind. Had I photographed him he would probably been annoyed, because Muslims object to being photographed, but in a drawing the result is visible at once.

The writers were very pleased with my portraits.

'We are in fact just flatterers!' said Paul, disgruntled. The Academy of Arts ordered portraits of all its members – about forty of them, and I accepted the commission because of the money, but it was not a success. However, I was able to draw others than just writers.

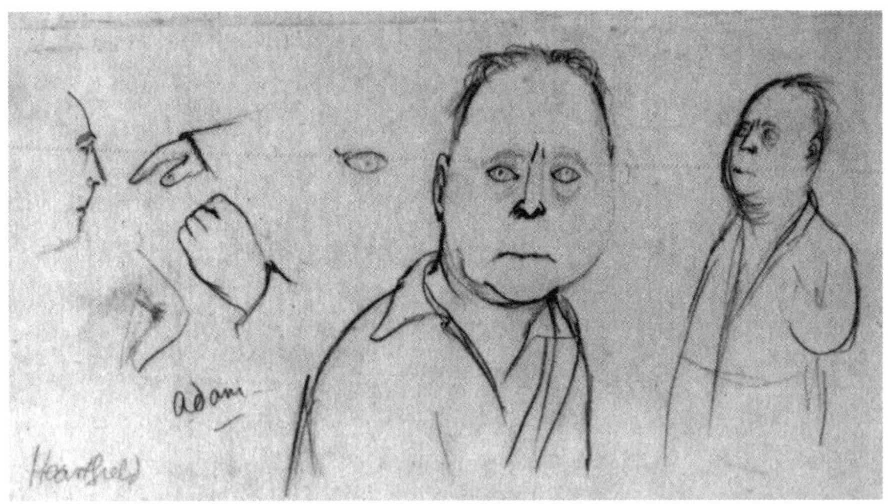

Sketches of John Heartfield.

'John Heartfield'.

I had met John Heartfield already in England. This gifted, simple and passionate person returned to Germany a little later than most of the political emigrants after the war, and he and his brother Wieland Herzfelde were received with some coolness by the authorities. Photomontage was classified as formalist, and if Brecht had not intervened, it would have been more disastrous for the brothers. Years later there was a major Heartfield exhibition in the National Gallery, and then it was obvious that even without the content he was a very great artist. But in those early days after the war, he must have been often very discouraged.

I remember that René and I were having lunch in the theatre club once when Johnny came past. 'I know what you have been saying about me!' he shouted at René as he passed with a furious glance, leaving us speechless and confounded. René was not always very diplomatic. 'Not everyone likes being slapped on the back!' said our friend Georg Honigmann. But René loved Johnny and his impulsive manner, which was so like his own. His unknown offence was later forgiven, and when our common friends the Carlines visited Berlin, we were invited to the Heartfield cottage on Scharmützelsee. Johnny hoisted the pastel-coloured Chinese silken flags as was his habit when visitors came. He was a strenuous host. When we went out for a dip in the lake in the early morning, Johnny appeared on the bank. 'Come on! Swim! Swim!' he urged us on. After breakfast a massive hunt for mushrooms in the forest was organized. 'Could we not buy them in a shop?' groaned Dick, as he was reproached for not searching hard enough.

Sketches of Hanns Eisler.

'Hanns Eisler'.

Commissioned by the Academy, I also visited Hanns Eisler. He opened a bottle of champagne at once, it foamed, Eisler sparkled, his pretty wife Steffie looked on. He was not a handsome man, and it was not easy to draw him, but at the last moment, as he accompanied me to the door and turned to go back to his room, I suddenly saw my drawing. My success in the field of portrait drawing led to a wave of other caricatures in this genre. First Sandberg, then Harald Kretzschmar in the magazine *Eulenspiegel*. From time to time I would be asked to do a portrait, but I had indigestion after my Academy series, and had actually lost interest in portraits. However, when the *Eulenspiegel* rang up and asked me to draw the old Yugoslav architect Selman Selmanagić, I agreed. He had been friendly with René, was also scarred in the formalist debate, and was surely easy to draw with his black eyes. I went along to their flat and found Selman and his good-looking wife little changed. He was, however, rather excited and confused. 'Yes, yes,' he said, 'René and I always had rows with each other! He was all for socialist realism …' 'You are mixing him up with someone else,' intervened his wife, but he took no notice. He went out of the room and came back with freshly combed hair. Even at eighty, vanity rules. He arranged himself in a pose on the sofa. 'Now you can begin!' he said to me. But I found him absolutely impossible to draw. I made a few notes. 'I'll finish it at home,' I said. Soon afterwards, Selman died.[1]

I did not take on any more commissions for portraits. I like drawing members of my family, but more in the style of the fine artists, than the caricaturists.

'Peter Huchel'.

At the time when I was busy with my writer caricatures, Brecht was still alive. I made sketches of him during rehearsals in the theatre, and his wife, Helene Weigel, tried to persuade me to bring a book of the caricatures of David Low to show to Brecht, who admired his work, but I was too shy. Shortly after the Writers' Congress, Brecht died. We were on holiday in Ahrenshoop on the Baltic coast at the time, together with the Uhses, the poet Stephan Hermlin, the sculptor Fritz Cremer and the French writers Francois and Martine Monod. When we received the news of Brecht's death, the men decided to return to Berlin for the funeral. We grass widows were to stay with the children. 'Come on,' said Christa Cremer, 'let's put on trousers and go dancing!' So when the children were in bed, off we went to Café Niemann. It was very full, but we found a table and were in high spirits. But although everyone rocked noisily round the clock, nobody asked us to dance, and so, strangely, we had nothing to confess next day.

'Gret Palucca'.

Not long afterwards, Helene Weigel asked me to illustrate some poems of Brecht for children, as yet unpublished. She wanted to make a small private edition on the occasion of Brecht's sixtieth birthday, which should not be sold in the shops, but distributed in the schools to the best pupils. I then had sessions with her during which we discussed the Brechtian approach to the illustration of them. The result was a slender volume which can occasionally be found in second-hand bookshops. Later Helene Weigel organized a matinee for children in the Schiffbauerdamm Theatre, based on the drawings and text in this little book. I performed a sort of circus act, drawing pictures on the stage while actors recited the poems. The layman has absolutely no idea how long it takes to complete a drawing, and it was only possible for me to keep pace with the actors when I marked in advance some points on the paper, which were invisible to the audience, and which enabled me to draw very rapidly by joining them up. Walking on to the stage was always an ordeal for me, but I was very proud to receive an actor's fee – and from the Berliner Ensemble!

Since my childhood in Belfast, I have always been crazy about the theatre. On our family holidays at the seaside, I attended all possible performances of the Pierrots, then a free open-air show in most resorts, always hoping that they would choose me when a child from the audience was required to step up and take part in some maudlin drama. But most of all I was fascinated by the various possibilities of transforming life into art on the stage.

About this time I first met Hans Bunge, who was in charge of the Brecht Archives at the time. He showed me the rooms in which Brecht had lived in the Chausseestraße, which were then not so tidied up as they are today. I made some sketches of the rocking chairs on which Brecht liked to sit and used them as vignettes in the little book of verses for children.

For a man with a chin like Bunge, there was no smooth path to success. Highly intelligent and extremely wilful, he had to overcome many hurdles and conflicts before he achieved success as a biographer with his books *Fragen Sie mehr über Brecht* [Do you have more questions about Brecht?], – *Brecht, Music and Culture: Hanns Eisler in Conversation with Hans Bunge*, and his book about Ruth Berlau, *Brechts Lai-tu*, the friend and collaborator of Brecht for many years. Hans Bunge came from a right-wing family and in his youth, he said, he was an enthusiastic member of the Hitler Youth movement. He only changed his opinions after meeting Brecht, when he came back to Germany after nine years in a Soviet prisoner-of-war camp. I had been many years in this country before I met one person who admitted to having been a Nazi. Bunge was an honest man.

'Brecht in a Rocking Chair, 1978'.

Illustration for Bertolt Brecht. *Ein Kinderbuch* [A Children's Book], 1965.[2]

Bertolt Brecht. *Ein Kinderbuch,* 1965. Title page.

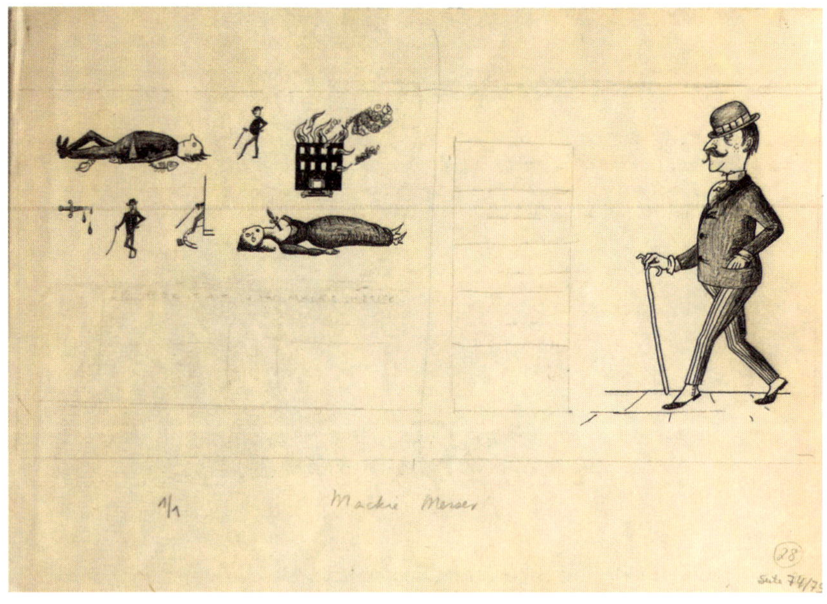

'Mack, the Knife'. Illustration for Bertolt Brecht. *Ein Kinderbuch,* 1965.

'If Sharks Were Men'. Illustration for Bertolt Brecht. *Ein Kinderbuch*, 1965.

'Mother Courage'. Illustration for Bertolt Brecht. *Ein Kinderbuch*, 1965.

9

Naturally, we had many friends among the foreigners in Berlin. The Cold War of the fifties resulted in an anti-communist campaign in the United States and the persecution of American communists and their sympathisers by the House of Un-American Activities Committee (HUAC). Many had to leave their country to avoid imprisonment, and moved to Paris, then some found refuge in the GDR. The singer Aubrey Pankey and his wife Kay, as well as the cartoonist Oliver Harrington took up residence in Berlin at this time. They had both been active in the movement for black equality in the United States. This generation of Americans, who had fought in the war against Germany had to overcome considerable unconscious barriers to merging with the country that had been the one-time enemy, which explains why after many years of residence, some spoke only halting German.

There were refugees from other countries too, like our friend the Greek poet Melpo Axioti, who was in Paris in 1948 when the right-wing colonels took over in Greece. She could not return and went to Poland, where she had been offered a job in the Greek department of the university, and then transferred to the Humboldt University in Berlin. She deliberately did not learn German, because she said that to learn yet another foreign language would damage her literary skill. She spoke French with her friends, and lived in a hotel in a transient lifestyle, learning only about enough German to say '*Ein Bier bitte!*' She was of course very isolated and lonely and when the chance came to return to Greece during a short break in the rules of the colonels, she did so. But not long afterwards they were back in power and she then retired to a small island in her beloved Aegean where she later died. I remember that we went with Melpo to hear Martin Luther King speak in a church in Berlin. When we arrived, there was no more room inside and the crowd seemed about to storm the gates until an official came out to announce that King would go on afterwards to address a second gathering in the Sophienkirche, so we all ran to the Sophienkirche where we sat in the pews and hymns were sung until he arrived. 'Never,' said Melpo, 'did I think I would see a revolution in Berlin!' The Maoist regime in China drove the American Jay Leyda out of Peking to the GDR with his wife, the dancer Si-Lan Chen. Jay was a distinguished expert on early Russian films, and he worked for several years in Berlin, building up the archives of the repertory Babylon cinema, before he was able to return to New York in the late 1960s, to take up a post in New York University. I had known the brother of his wife when he lived in London during the war. He was an artist called Jack Chen and they came from an interesting family. Their father had been foreign minister at the time of Sun-Yat-sen, and his three children were a mixture of Russian, Jamaican and Chinese physiognomy. Si-Lan was delicately built and frail, Jack looked sturdy and Chinese, Yolanda, who was married to a film producer in Moscow, looked very Jamaican. One of Jay's difficulties was that the American authorities denied Si-Lan a residence permit in New York, but they managed to get it in the end, and I last saw Si-Lan in their apartment in Washington Square, where she sat, dressed in a long robe, with that strange immobility of a dancer not in motion, in an empty neutral room, which suggested impermanency, as did their flat in Berlin.

From China too came Alan Winnington, who had spent twelve years there. At the end of the Korean War, he and our old friend Wilfred Burchett lost their passports as a result of having reported for the North Korean side and could not return home. When the anti-foreign campaign began in Peking, Alan was posted as *Daily Worker* correspondent to Berlin. Alan was tall and cheerful, and a welcome addition to our foreign community because he brought the Chinese cuisine with him, as well as that wonderful London humour and unsentimentality, which endeared him to me. He had no inhibitions about learning German. He mixed with the Berliners and wrote detective stories to make his life as an expatriate more interesting and remunerative.

Opening of the Sachsenhausen Memorial, with Jean Effel, 1961.

John Peet was the other English newspaperman in East Berlin. He had been a correspondent for Reuters News Agency, and he said that his reports on West German rearmament were not printed in England so in 1950 he demonstratively left West Berlin for the GDR. Here he edited and produced a little weekly news-sheet in English, *German Democratic*

Report, which for twenty-five years gave a readable resumé of events from a GDR standpoint. As the GDR was then aiming at diplomatic recognition, this was very useful to them. As soon as this recognition was achieved, the authorities found a pretext to withdraw his publication licence. John then lived by translation. Alan was a party man and had the backing of an organization when he needed support. Apart from the Veterans Association of the Spanish International Brigade, John did not belong to any party. Therefore, no one saw to it that better use was made of his knowledge and experience accumulated during an adventurous life. Tall and thin, he wore a varied selection of whiskers and often looked like a stage Englishman, until at the end he wore a long straggling beard, as if he had taken on the role of an eccentric, and which maybe fitted with the bitterness he must have felt.

Our Italian friend the painter Gabriele Mucchi, had a flat in Berlin, but was not seeking refuge. He had close links with the city since his first wife, the sculptress Genni, had been German and he knew Berlin since the thirties. For a time, he taught painting in the art school, continued to visit regularly from Milan, and exhibited his work here as well as there. He built a bridge between Italy and the GDR for the artists who often benefitted from his generous invitations. Typical of Mucchi's great charm and vitality is his reaction during the opening of an exhibition of his work and Genni's in the *Kloster Unser Lieben Frauen* in Magdeburg. There were several long-drawn-out formal speeches by various functionaries, which made the audience restive. Then Gabriele rose to speak.

'I had intended,' he said, 'to speak to you about realism in art, but as the last speaker talked for such a long time, I decided to sing a song instead!' And he sang an Italian song, and as the acoustic was so good he sang another one in his fine voice, so remarkable for a man of eighty-eight.

Mucchi could return to Italy when he wished, which was as well, for he was very Italian. His compatriot, the Venetian Casanova, wrote in his memoirs that, while banished in Trieste, 'I was suffering from nostalgia, what the Swiss and Germans call "*Heimweh*" and the French "*Mal du Pays*." "*Heimweh*" is a mortal disease; for I verily believe I should have died of homesickness had I not at last been able to return and spend nine years in the bosom of the country which had always proved such a cruel stepmother to me.'

I think that all those foreigners I knew felt at some time that piercing pain of homesickness, which is bound to afflict those who live away from the community in which they grew up. In the world today it is not rare that people are forced to leave their countries. They tend then to live in ethnic communities until their children merge with the local population. For the individual who has taken up residence in a foreign country it is not easy, but there are positive aspects to this situation. It teaches flexibility and tolerance and freedom from the bondage of nationality, with its ingrained prejudices, should be a humanizing element.

Elizabeth Shaw with Gabriele Mucchi, 1978.

10

In 1952 we went on holiday to the Baltic coast for the first time. At first it did not seem like the sea to us, because there was no tide, and green grass growing almost to the edge of the water. We stayed in the village of Kloster on the island of Hiddensee, gently undulating slopes with small white cottages dotted on them, children with Nordic flaxen hair, and no traffic at all. No cars were allowed then, and the island could only be reached by steamer from Stralsund.

'Windswept Trees in Ahrenshoop, at the German Baltic Sea'.

After this pleasant experience we went to the Baltic on holiday almost every year, but mostly to the traditional artists' resort of Ahrenshoop on the mainland, where holiday places could be booked through that kind institution, the League of Culture. Ahrenshoop had been an artist's resort since about the turn of the century because painters were attracted by the remarkable light, which resulted from two stretches of water on each side of a narrow strip of land. In the fifties it was still difficult to reach, as most of us still did not have cars. We took the train to Rostock, and then, grabbing children and luggage, ran across the platform to catch the small local train to Ribnitz, where we changed to a rather temperamental bus, and bumped along a road full of potholes until the road ended and the Darss forest began, and there was Ahrenshoop, still mainly a fishing village.

The League of Culture in Berlin, which distributed the holiday places, sometimes gave us beds at the bakery, sometimes at the hairdresser or the post office. We only found out when we got there. We could wander along the village street in a bathrobe, for it was a quiet place. In the evening, cowbells tinkled as the cows were driven home from pasture, and after a day on the beach we repaired to the Kurhaus to meet friends and join in great battles about whether nude bathing should be allowed or not and cultural and political matters of the day, besides which we played cards, gossiped, flirted and rocked around the clock. Since those carefree days, a road to Stralsund has been built through Ahrenshoop and traffic roars through, making it more dangerous on a bicycle than in Berlin. The cultured have acquired weekend country residences, where they are busy mowing their own lawns and have no time for those innocent fiery disputes we pursued so passionately in the fifties.

'Ahrenshoop in Winter'.

II

About this time, the editor of the small monthly *Das Magazin*, modelled at first on the English *Lilliput*, suggested that the writer Berta Waterstradt and I travel round the country and report in a light-hearted manner on various towns and villages, I drawing sketches, she writing verses. I did not know Berta very well. I had done a caricature of her for a series during a writers' congress, and she felt insulted and screamed at me quite publicly in the press club. However, we set off for Rostock on our first trip together, amicably discussing our approach to the commission. Berta suggested that we should invent a young couple who travel together but remembering a reportage I had done with Arnold Rattenbury for *Our Time* in London, I proposed that the two characters could be ourselves.

After a time, we developed a certain routine on our trips. I left the choice of the town to the editorial department or Berta, as I did not know the country so well. Our journeys usually took place in poor weather because the magazine found it impossible to get a hotel booking for us in the holiday season. When we arrived at our destination, we went to the tourist information bureau – if there was one – then to the bookshop and local library to obtain information and brochures. It was always useful to have the name of someone living there to get an inside view of the place. In the evening we then jotted down six or seven principal features that should be included in our portrait of a place – say, the castle, the marketplace and some special feature. The next day we separated. I went to sketch, mostly in fog, wind and rain, which made the sketches cursory, but I used to buy postcards, if available, so that I could check on details when doing the finished drawings at home. In the meantime, Berta sat mostly in cafés and pondered. She sought an '*Aufhänger*', as she called it, a particular characteristic, which would provide title and verse. In the evening we met again and compared progress. If Berta had already composed some verses, she read them out and we matched them to my sketches.

The next day the same procedure, and then we went back to Berlin where Berta completed her text and sent it to me so that I could finish the drawings and deliver the job to the editorial department.

Probably this popular reportage by two women is quite unique. It continued for about twenty years, at irregular intervals, and gave me the opportunity of visiting many places I would not otherwise have seen. Not only did I learn a lot about the geography of the country, but Berta told me something about the history, about her Jewish background, and the two years she spent in jail under the Nazis.

'Jail is not so bad,' she said, 'once you know the ropes and get used to the routine.' The first thing she wanted when she was released was a big slice of creamy cake. Her husband, who was not Jewish, refused to divorce her and stood by her till the war was over, when he took another and left her very sharp-tongued about the male sex, as indeed about everything else. As we travelled together, we got to know each other well and to respect our boundaries. Berta, with her earthy approach to life, always made me laugh, and I like people who make me laugh. I need them.

Our excursions were mostly to places in the GDR, but sometimes abroad, for instance to Kattowitz in Poland, which was Berta's birthplace, and so on the return journey from Cracow, where we had spent a few days, we alighted at Kattowitz station. We wanted to have a look at her former home, and so we took the tram to a part of the town, which seemed to be untouched by the war. Berta led me to a house in the corner of a quiet square. 'That is it!' she said, turned abruptly, went to a newspaper kiosk and bought a picture postcard of the town for her sister in Israel. We passed her old school, just round the corner, rather rapidly, and did not go in because she did not care for her schooldays, she said. 'Now I'll show you where I got my first kiss!' We went into a café and ordered coffee and a kind of chocolate bun, which was on the menu then and now. This trip to Kattowitz could have been considered a sentimental journey, but Berta disguised it with another task, the search for an electric heater, unobtainable in the GDR, but which we found in Kattowitz and bore home triumphantly. The writer Günter Kunert wrote in an article entitled 'We like Berta,':

> Berta, absolutely earthbound, without any metaphysical iridescence, nothing wondrous or eccentric about her appears sometimes to be a small edition of the long non-existent symbol of the city: Berolina, Berta and Berlin reveal themselves to be synonymous: matter-of-fact and practical; determined not to be got down; healthy Chutzpah and cool wit, combined with sensitivity, as Tucholsky described it, the classical Berliner type of combined sympathy and cheekiness – from Kattowitz, of course …

Berlin is poorer without Berta.

Spreewald is a district south of Berlin inhabited by the only national minority in the GDR, the Slavonic Sorbs[1] who have their own language and sometimes put on picturesque peasant costumes. The river Spree splits there into many streams and the inhabitants communicate by boat through a marshy region. It is a favourite resort for outings from Berlin, and the editorial department of *Das Magazin* suggested that Berta and I should do one of our little reportages on it. They provided us with a car and driver from the firm for our convenience.

The driver picked me up first. He arrived late and his eyes looked glazed. We gave Patrick a lift to work and there was no conversation. The driver had difficulty in understanding where Patrick wanted to be dropped. Afterwards he told us he had driven 'Hilde' to Thuringia and back the day before, a long day, and a wonder that the 'old box' had stood the journey.

He told me that all the cars in *Das Magazin* were very old. He had been driving exclusively for the paper for a month now, referring chummily to 'Hilde' and 'Manfred' with the innocence of one who has only been there for a month. I wonder if he calls her so to her face.

We hooted at Berta's place, and eventually she emerged. She sat on the front seat and engaged the driver in conversation. I noticed that she was also a little taken aback by his reference to 'Hilde'. 'How is René?' she asked over her shoulder, 'He has not thanked my sister for the picture she sent him from Israel!' 'Oh yes! He has done so now.' 'Has he hung the picture?' 'Of course. In his studio,' I lied. I knew that Berta was bursting with gossip and questions as always, but she was holding herself in check until we should be rid of the third party, the driver. In the meantime she pumped him for news of Hilde and wanted to know some details about the private life of the editor of the paper he had last driven for, but was frustrated there, for he had only driven for the staff.

She also asked him about the town of Finsterwalde, famous for its singers, which was in the neighbourhood of Spreewald. Berta decided that we would first stop at Lübbenau and do a trip on the river; then drive to the hotel, where she would have a rest and then she and I would spend the rest of the day alone, gossiping and seeing the sights. Next day to Cottbus. But of course, when we arrived in Lübbenau – breakfast first! We found a café on the waterfront. 'I'll have a pot of coffee, a boiled egg and two rolls. You'll have tea, and you, Meister?' 'I'll have a pot of coffee and an egg,' said I, to be provoking. 'And I'll have an omelette,' said the driver. 'Well if you are all going to have such exotic things,' said Berta, slightly off course, 'Then I'll have scrambled eggs and ham.' Mine took a long time to come, and Berta was sharpish with the rather sleepy waitress, who did not know when the boats go either.

We went outside, where long punts were drawn up on the edge of the river and went into an office to ask when the boating trips took place. We were told that we could join one at about eleven. Outside, however, the punts were filling up already with schoolchildren and Berta insisted that we must find room in one of them, and so we did, all three sitting together, with Berta in the middle. We set off. The punter, an old man with a saucy nautical cap, was just behind us, and kept up a flow of patter: 'You children, what about a song? You children, take a photo from the back of the boat. One step backwards and it will be even better! Ha, ha!' We moved forwards in a convoy of punts through narrow waterways. It was extremely cold and windy, but the scenery was pretty. April green, cottages, fields and overhanging willows, storks nesting.

From *Das Magazin*.

From *Das Magazin*.

Occasionally we met another boat, farmers on their business. The tourist season had scarcely begun. The picturesque Spreewald costume had been replaced by rubber boots and pullovers and the punts were unromantically affixed with engines. On them old ladies sat hunched up with baskets, going shopping, their sons with a piece of machinery for farm work. The notices on the shore were in German, Sorbian and Polish. Eventually we landed at a restaurant, which was shut, and at a museum, which did not interest Berta, though she gave it a formal glance. However, she did manage to transmit some scandalous gossip as we walked along for a few minutes, ahead of the driver. We did a ten-minute tour of the tiny village and Berta and the driver dived into the tiny grocery shop, with true Berliner instinct, to see if there was anything worth having. Berta bought a small packet of chocolate biscuits. Little did we know how they would be appreciated later on. Then with our twenty or so noisy boat-rocking children, we punted slowly back to Lübbenau. It was very cold, and we did not feel expansive.

Conversation was brief. We decided, shivering, to drive straight to Finsterwalde. Three hours on the river gave us an appetite for a nice schnapps and a chat. In the car we could warm up a bit.

Eighteen miles from Finsterwalde, on a lonely road, the car began to hiccup strangely, and we stopped, the driver examined the engine but could not find the fault. He stood out in the cold wind, unscrewing this and that and expressing uncertainty about the future. 'Maybe we should walk back to the autobahn and thumb a lift,' he suggested. Berta sat tight inside and said no. She was too old to thumb lifts. No one would take her.

'Well, what do you think we should do?' I asked, 'I don't know. It is the driver's fault. He should have checked the car instead of coming with us on the boat trip.' I was not for the hitching idea because it was quite far to the autobahn, and I had a huge portfolio with me, which I wanted to deliver to a gallery in Dresden. At last, a car passed, and we stopped it, and the two drivers talked about engine trouble and we learned that it was not the road to Finsterwalde anyway. The cold wind blew over the green fields between lines of forest and our driver's nose dripped. Finally, he screwed everything back and we began to crawl along in the direction we had been shown, hoping to reach a main road, where we might get a lift. 'There may be some kind of explosion,' warned the driver cautiously. 'You mean that we may be blasted into the air?' I asked frivolously. The driver did not reply, which alarmed me a little, and Berta more so. She said later that the conversation made her heart beat wildly. *Back to Berlin,* was her only thought. Already days before, she said, she was dreading the trip. And never again by car. We would go by train, where we could talk freely about this and that, without the burden of a no-good, incompetent, lazy driver.

We made it. We found the hotel. It had a restaurant, and the rooms were not bad. *Das Magazin* had forgotten to book a bed for the driver, though. That pleased Berta. Firstly, she had an excuse to rant about the inhumanity and negligence of the editorial department, and secondly, she could not care less about the driver. We went downstairs and ordered lunch, leaving him to telephone Berlin. He finally appeared to say that a car was coming to tow him back later in the afternoon. 'You can go back with him,' I suggested to Berta, and she readily agreed. The thought that she would be tucked up in her own safe bed tonight cheered her up at once. I decided to stay the night in the hotel and go on to Dresden the next day. Berta went upstairs to lie down for an hour while I checked trains at the station.

Then we went for a stroll in the little town. To the bookshop, where we found nothing to buy. Down to the pretty little red town hall. We could not find a brochure about the town, but we saw a notice which indicated that there was a library in the town hall. Berta introduced us to the librarian and told her what we were looking for. The composer of the famous song, '*Die Sänger von Finsterwalde*' [The Singer from Finsterwalde], was still alive, and we could interview him. She gave us his address and said everyone could direct us to it. Outside we asked a pleasant-looking boy the way, but he did not speak German. '*Polski?*' asked Berta. '*Russki,*' said he. We asked another passer-by, but strangely he didn't speak German either. Eventually a woman showed us the way. The composer and his wife were at home. They were very old, but just about to leave to go to the circus, which was the big event in Finsterwalde that day, as I had noticed on a poster. 'Frau Shaw will draw a portrait of you first!' announced Berta. A little startled,

I took out pencil and paper, but the old pair hastily produced photographs, which I could take with me – the circus was waiting! We departed. Back in the hotel, the second driver had arrived. Berta bid driver number one bring her bags down, and I bade them all farewell and wished a safe journey home.

I went to the local cinema and saw Marlon Brando in *The Man in the Snakeskin*.[2] There was a sparse audience of businessmen, like me looking for an evening's entertainment. Finsterwalde is a dormitory town for Cottbus. The film was grim Tennessee Williams. I had a feeling of fear – maybe the film or the name of the town induced it – and was glad to get back to the hotel and lock the door. Next morning it was raining. I looked at the town again and made a few sketchy notes. The hotel restaurant was shut, and I breakfasted in a restaurant called '*Sängerstadt*' on the marketplace. I looked at the little castle, which was being renovated. There was a garden round the moat. Along the street were wide old doors, sixteenth or seventeenth century. About this time there must have been a good ironsmith working there, as there was a variety of fine door handles, each one different.

I went early to the station and sat there reading and thinking how little it had altered since 1880. On by train to Großenhain. Lunch in the station and read on. To Dresden, taxi to Kupferstichkabinett, where I handed in the portfolio. Back to the station and train to Berlin. Arrived home. Nasty shock for René and Patrick, who had bought lots of *Blutwurst* and leeks and things I don't like, and were settling down to have a nice time, poor things.

12

Karl Gossow, who was in charge of book design in the Aufbau Verlag, always urged me to illustrate children's books. I did this too, but often found the texts I was given of such bad quality that I thought I could do better myself. At the beginning of the sixties our financial situation was as usual at a low ebb, so that we had to give back some holiday places because we could not pay for them, and so I dashed off the stories *Der kleine Angsthase* [The Timid Rabbit] and *Gittis Tomatenpflanze* [Gitti's Tomato Plant]. The first one, I told the children, is to get some money now, as we need it, and the second one is for later. However, being greedy and impatient, I gave them both up together. The Kinderbuchverlag was a little worried about the element of caricature, which was new then, and the amount of white space, but the public received the books eagerly and asked for more. After that, our financial problems were solved, and I was mainly known as a maker of children's books.

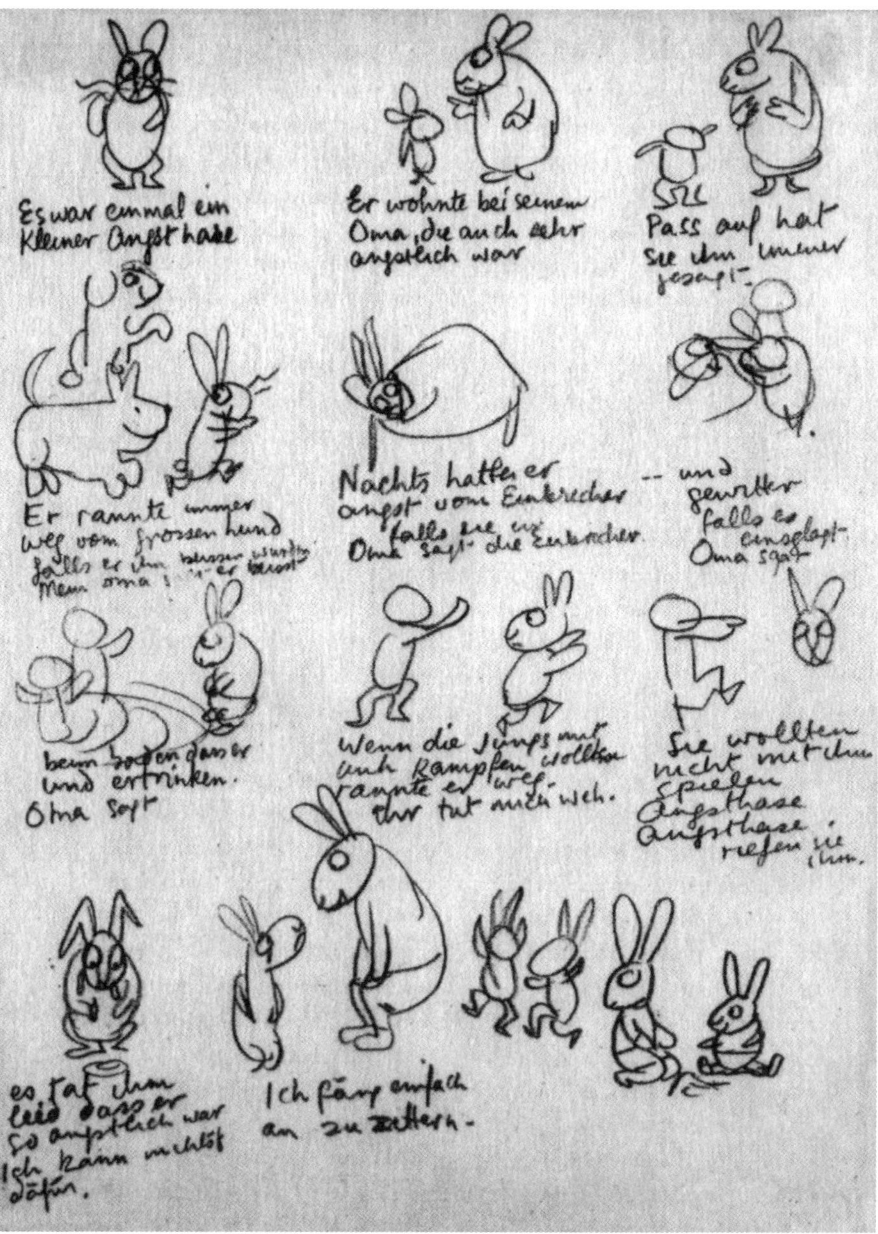

First sketches for *Der kleine Angsthase* [The Timid Rabbit].

Illustration from *Der kleine Angsthase.*

Illustration from *Der kleine Angsthase.*

Illustration from *Der kleine Angsthase.*

Illustration from *Der kleine Angsthase.*

Illustration from *Der kleine Angsthase.*

I have often wondered why my children's books were so popular. I finished the books, gave them up, and got on with the next one without looking at them again, once they were published. Once, however, I was persuaded to read one to a school class in Schwerin, during a book fair there. It was *Bettina bummelt* [Bettina Strolls], and two classes had been squeezed into the desks to hear this moral tale. No sooner had I begun to read than the children were convulsed with giggles. This was not because of the famous Shaw humour, but because of my funny accent, which was new in Schwerin. Order was restored with frowns and rebukes from the teachers, but as I continued to read, I realized that this was a terrible story, which I did not like at all, but I could not stop now and had to continue to the bitter end. I have never read to a class since and avoid looking at my past work if I can help it.

Sometimes I have been asked whether I wrote my children's books for my own children, but they were in fact past the picture-book age when I began. When I first tried to think of an idea, I tried to remember how I felt as a child, and how often I was afraid, and so I wrote *Der kleine Angsthase.* I remembered how I had longed for a garden when we lived in Belfast, and so *Gittis Tomatenpflanze* came about. An idea was often brewing at the back of my mind for a long time, either a theme or a character, before it crystallized into a book. I wrote mostly very moral tales, trying to put across certain values such as courage, kindness and living for something bigger than oneself, because I have this missionary spirit that prompted me to do political cartoons. Anyway, children are very moral too and have a strong sense of justice until it is dispersed by the adult world. Some of my stories are just fun, because adults are often so solemn and children like fun. Once I saw an old Italian grandpa sitting in a clothes store in Berlin and translating one of my books for his grandchild, both laughing heartily. That pleased me greatly.

Some say that my style is always the same – having found a readable formula, line and watercolour, I stay with it. Artistic experiments take place in other fields.

Illustration from *Gittis Tomatenpflanze* [Gitti's Tomato Plant].

Illustration from *Bella Belchaud und ihre Papageien*
[Bella Belchaud and her Parrots].

Illustration from *Bella Belchaud und ihre Papageien.*

13

I have always had something to do with children. In the clannish family in which I grew up, there were always the big and small ones and, with luck, a baby around. My maternal instinct must have been apparent, and Granny designated me as the one who should wash the small faces in the evening and put the children to bed. I liked doing this because I then had an appreciative audience for my long stories, invented on the spot. My mother wished very much that I would take up nursery-school teaching as a career. There was a training college just round the corner in Bedford and she would have kept me in the neighbourhood, leading a life without stress that she thought would be best for me, instead of going off to London and the arts.

We mothers tend to be overprotective towards our children. It is difficult to realize that they have to give us a kick to overcome Oedipus and Electra complexes and to expand to their full size. We have to get used to having them and we have to learn to let them go.

Our children, growing up in the GDR with both parents foreigners, had to establish an identity of their own. They wanted to be like everyone else around them. They spoke with a strong Berliner dialect, and tried to get us to conform to the customs of the country. They patiently explained that when their friends came to supper, there had to be forks on the table. 'What! Forks for bread and sausage?' I asked, amazed. 'Last time they asked whether we were very poor, because there was a jug of water to drink!' I was informed. Our children introduced us to strange rigid German customs like '*Kaffee trinken*', which seems to be regarded by some as a law of nature. 'You really don't drink coffee in the afternoon? Ah, tea perhaps?'

And birthdays. In Britain birthdays are sometimes celebrated in a casual way, but in Germany they belong to a lifelong solemn ritual. The birthday table must be heaped with flowers and presents, and there must be at least three sorts of cake, or else you are not loved enough. The grandeur and importance of birthdays increases with each decade, and should you not want to admit your age, this is considered very coy. Anyway, in the GDR it was impossible because everyone was obliged to carry an identity card, to be produced on demand. This card is issued to young citizens, who have reached the age of fourteen, in a solemn civil ceremony resembling confirmation in the church.

It was not easy for our children to grow up in a country where both parents were unfamiliar with the customs and traditions. They followed the conservative East German pattern of life first to kindergarten, then to school when they were six years old. They joined the Young Pioneers, then the Free German Youth movement. It was not strictly compulsory to join these organizations, but it was expected. After leaving school they went their individual ways, choosing their own careers and partners.

My daughter Anne, my firstborn, was very robust, in spite of her premature birth, and was rarely ill. Fortunately, she was good at school, because we were not able to help much with homework when it was German grammar, or Russian, which was the first foreign language, or indeed German history. She read a great deal, was affectionate and sensitive. She was a long time with us at home because she studied the English language at the Humboldt University in Berlin. She married and had her first child while she was still a student. Her husband was still studying too, in Rostock, and so we had the pleasure of a little grandchild at home, before she moved up north to Mecklenburg to join her husband. René drove her and her daughter to their new address. 'I never knew it would be so hard to leave home!' she said, as we hugged each other. I had mentioned to her that René did not like to feel that he was being used as a chauffeur, and so on parting she tearfully handed him a present of a pair of socks. 'These are my socks of love!' said he, when he returned to Berlin.

I always found the various stages of children's growing independence painful and difficult. Patrick, the second, was prone to infection. He was a charming child, lively, humorous and outgoing. He had a frail nervous system and when his temperature rose rapidly, usually at the onset of some infection, he was liable to go into convulsions. The first time this happened I was terrified. The car from the editorial department called to take me to work and we drove to hospital instead. Another time I was working at home when a very distressed kindergarten assistant came to ask me to come at once. The children attended a little kindergarten just round the corner. Patrick lay there quite inert. An ambulance was called, and I went with him to the hospital. He looked at me silently, wearily, then his eyes slowly closed. I thought he was dead, and cried out, 'Patrick!' Startled, he opened his eyes at once. Fortunately, these fits were outgrown by the time he went to school. At school he had bad luck with his teachers. It was in the 1950s and the East–West border was still open. Twice his class teacher was suddenly absent. They had both left for the West. '*Sie ist abgehauen* [She has pushed off]?' I exclaimed, on hearing the news. '*Es heißt nicht abgehauen*,' corrected Patrick, 'It's not called pushing off, it's called changing her place of residence to the West!'

Patrick was always good company. Sometimes we went on little excursions to town together. Once, when he was about eight, I suggested that we should visit the Natural History Museum and see the animals. He assented cheerfully, but when we went in, he looked around in dismay. 'But they are all dead!' he said, 'how did they die?' 'Oh, they got to be very old and died, and then they were stuffed,' I lied guiltily. 'And these?' said Patrick indignantly, pointing to a nest of stuffed hamsters, babes and all. We felt an urgent need to get out of this awful graveyard. The attendant spoke to us as we left. 'Round the corner you'll find the birds of prey. That's something for the boy!' he said jovially. We went to the geology department and looked for some time at the collection of stones, jagged and glittering, smooth and coloured, soothing.

Patrick was always compassionate and quick to detect injustice. After school he did a course in market research, but soon realized that it was not his line and moved into the field of education, taking a diploma in the training of physically disabled children and working in a model school in Berlin.

My grandchildren have at least one really German parent, and German relatives, so their lives are not so complicated by problems of identity. The two older ones have grown up on the edge of a big lake, north of Berlin, and speak in the singing tones of Mecklenburg. The youngest lives in Berlin, and sometimes I go for a walk with him, and sometimes our adventures result in a children's book. It is nice to be a wise old grandmother. I note that the parents think they can direct their children's lives, and I know that they cannot. My grandchildren are a great source of fun and happiness to me.

14

So, we'll go no more a roving
So late into the night,
Though the heart be still as loving,
And the moon be still as bright.

For the sword outwears its sheath,
And the soul wears out the breast,
And the heart must pause to breathe,
And love itself have rest.

Though the night was made for loving,
And the day returns too soon,
Yet we'll go no more a roving
By the light of the moon.

George Gordon, Lord Byron 1788–1824

At the beginning of the sixties the Cold War resulted in the closing of the frontier between West Berlin and the German Democratic Republic. The Wall was built. It had been long expected that something of the kind would happen because of the number of people leaving the country. They would study in the East and then go to the West to get a job, where conditions were more amenable. It was clear that the GDR could not afford this strain on its resources.

We were living in Niederschönhausen then, and when we heard the news, we went down to Wollankstraße to see for ourselves and watched the Wall go up, brick by brick, weeping grannies waving handkerchiefs on both sides, until the Wall rose above them. For the politicians it seemed a rational solution, for the old Berliners it was a tragedy. lt was not the first wall in the world. The ancient Romans built one between England and Scotland, and there is the famous Wall of China. Wall Street in New York is named after the wall the Dutch built to keep the British out. But a wall through the middle of a modern city is only possible in Berlin, with a population resigned to defeat. A visible silent sign that this was a focal point of a worldwide conflict took place a little later, during a dispute over the right of allied troops to enter eastern territory, when a Soviet tank and an American one stood facing each other in the Friedrichstraße, only a few yards apart.

When the time comes for the history of the GDR to be written from the point of view of individual and social psychology, only then can one comprehend the extent and effect of this wall on the people. The division between East and West was the cause of a widespread schizophrenia. People who lived in the East took part in its social rituals; in the evening they switched on the television and looked West. Very few could travel to the West for business reasons. If they could then it was taboo to talk about it. It could also endanger their possibility of travelling abroad again. It led to what one psychiatrist called 'the Wall sickness', increasing depression, frustration and aggression.

When one counts the dead, who in desperation tried to escape and were shot by the frontier guards, one should also remember those, mostly young people, who suffered from psychic disturbance and took their own lives. It was some time before we realized the effect of the changed circumstances on us personally. I could no longer go to England with the children every year, as I was in the habit of doing. I was glad at least that I had kept my passport. Everyone likes to feel that they are free to travel, even if they do not want to at the moment.

At an exhibition of GDR children's books in London, 1967.

I suppose I inherited the urge to travel from my father. Before the First World War, when he was a bachelor, he saved all his money to go on holidays abroad, to Italy, North Africa, Norway, Finland and so on. Once, when returning from a holiday in Scandinavia, he realized as they crossed over the North Sea, that they were late, and he would hardly reach Liverpool in time to catch the steamer to Belfast and be at work the next morning. In desperation he sent off a telegram, 'Hold steamer, am delayed. Shaw.' Now the owner of the shipping line was called Shaw, and so sailing was delayed until my father came hurrying up the gangway with his old Gladstone bag and thanked the frowning captain for his consideration.

Those were the days when one barely needed a passport for travel, only to be compared with the confusion just after the Second World War, when the vast variety of travel documents enabled one man I heard of to travel half round the world on a Turkish menu, bound in red leather. 'The first thing,' he said, 'is to procure or forge a Swiss frontier stamp, and after that they'll all stamp it, the more the better!'

My father used to show my mother photographs of all the places he had been and promised they would go there together one day. Then three children were born in rapid succession and put an end to such dreams. When we were five, four and three, however, our parents went to Germany, travelling on a steamer down the Rhine to Mainz, to stay with Uncle John, who was British consul there. We were deposited with Granny, but first my mother told me that they were going to the Black Forest, which was full of fairies, and in case she should meet one, I should tell her if I had a wish, and she would pass it on. Tell her, I remember saying, that I don't want to grow up. I remember this great fear, an awareness of time passing, overcame me on my fourth birthday. I am not quite sure whether the fairy granted my wish or not, but our parents came back with a solid doll's house for us girls, found in the Black Forest, we were told.

Although exotic foreign trips were not practical for a large family, we rented a house for a month every summer on the English or Scottish coast. A big black trunk, a square greenish one and the old Gladstone bag stood on the corridor weeks before and were slowly packed with all that was necessary, until finally a grand expedition set forth, including odd cousins, aunts, the maid and great-aunt Fanny with her extraordinary hats as well. Before we left, a guidebook to our destination was studied and discussed, as if we were reporters about to cover it for *Das Magazin*!

Elizabeth Shaw, René Graetz and granddaughter Katrin, 1973.

15

Now we in the GDR had to adapt ourselves to the new confined conditions. We went for family holidays on the Black Sea coast of Bulgaria where there was sunshine and garlic, the Mediterranean of the East. René and I had the opportunity to travel for professional reasons. In 1964 the Chilean painter Venturelli arranged that he should go to Cuba for three months to help build up a printing workshop for the artists there. He travelled by sea on a merchant ship and came back with an enormous bunch of dried Cuban plants, coral gathered on the beach, and numerous tales of his adventures.

At the beginning of the sixties our good friend Richard Carline passed through Berlin, and we discussed the possibility of forming a national committee of AIAP, the UNESCO artists' organization in the GDR. This was done and René played a leading part in it.

His many languages and his experience in different countries were excellent qualifications for international work. Later he was voted president of the national committee. He now had ample opportunity to travel, and he spent a pleasant few weeks in Japan, attending a congress, and made a number of sketches. Carline, the Englishman, demanded eggs and bacon for breakfast. René preferred to live Japanese style.

Wherever he went, René adapted himself to the lifestyle of the country. In England he carried an umbrella, wore a flower in his buttonhole, and assumed a gentlemanly manner. When we travelled by train over the Bernese Oberland to visit his relatives in Geneva, he became more Swiss with every kilometre we covered. In Paris he dunked his croissant in the coffee and was absolutely French. French was his most perfect language. We spoke English at home, and he usually made notes in English or French.

Illustration from *Drei Mann in einem Boot, vom Hunde ganz zu schweigen* [Three Men in a Boat], 1967.

As the years passed, René concentrated much more on his work and seemed to be gathering confidence. He went his own way in experiments with form in sculpture and printing, as well as in methods of printing graphics that were not generally known among his colleagues. In all his work he aimed to express the great social conflicts of his time, sometimes in lyrical, sometimes monumental style. He was an innately social being, and the isolation into which he was sometimes forced during disputes on art theory were for him intensely painful. Not long before his death in 1974 he noted in a sketchbook that he knew at last what he wanted to do in art. René died suddenly while he was on a cure in a health resort in Graal-Müritz on the Baltic coast. I was extremely shaken when I received the news in Berlin, and it took me some time to realize that it was true. Nature helped with the curious therapy of dreams, in which we met, talked, sometimes quarrelled, and in which our life together continued in a strange fashion. I had to organize and arrange the art works he left behind, and I was increasingly impressed by his enormous productive energy and the extent of his work.

16

René and I lived together for more than thirty years. We were very different in background and in temperament but with both of us material possessions were not a priority. Perhaps we were a little careless. We both led our own lives and worked in a different style, if the same profession.

The fact that we did not have children at the time of our move to Germany probably made the decision easier. I had wished and I intended to have them earlier, but shortly after we married in 1944 I had a tubal pregnancy, which ruptured with lasting consequences. It was the time when the V-1 flying bombs began. I was an air-raid warden then, and when the sirens sounded at night I leapt out of bed, put on my thick navy warden's coat and helmet and ran down to the wardens post at the end of the road. On this particular evening I was not on duty, but the frequent flashes and noise of the attack prompted us to join the neighbours in the primitive shelter in the street, because we feared that if our house were hit, the gas pipes would burst. While we stood there I was seized with a violent pain and could just about hobble upstairs when the all-clear was sounded. The next day it was still there and when I stood up I fainted, much to René's concern. A doctor was called, and I was sent into New End Hospital, at the top of Hampstead Hill, treated for a miscarriage and told that I could go home two days later. René came to collect me, but halfway down the hill we had to get a taxi, because the pain was back and I could not walk.

The next day I was transported back to the hospital and a pregnancy in the ovarian tube was diagnosed. René had gone over to Carline's for company in the air raids and only later when he rang the hospital did he realize that they were waiting anxiously for his permission to operate on me. As they wheeled me in, the air-raid siren went, and I, half-doped, was just aware enough to hope that the surgeon's knife would not tremble.

All went well, however, though I had to spend six weeks in the ward, recovering from peritonitis. The morning after the operation the surgeon came in and, with the appearance of utmost concern, inquired: 'How is your husband?' René had interviewed him when he came up to the hospital and uttered terrifying threats if anything went wrong. The hospitals were being cleared quickly just then to make way for expected casualties from the V-1 air attacks. In the large ward where I lay, there were only very old ladies, and a few urgent cases like mine. One old lady of ninety had just had a leg taken off, and she was allowed to have her mug of beer in the evening, which she always raised to wish us all good health, a shy smile on her friendly face. There were big windows along both sides of the room, and we were told to put pillows over our faces when the air-raid warning sounded, in case of flying glass. Only one bomb dropped in the neighbourhood and it landed in a pond, near our house. René was in the bath when he heard it coming down and dived instinctively under the water. When I was let out of the hospital, René and I went to Bedford to stay with my parents, so that I could convalesce. I gave up my job in the factory and began to work at home as a serious freelance artist for *Lilliput* and for Fore Publications, where the designer Henrion[1] was art editor. Henrion, a refugee from Germany, invited me out to lunch with him, and told me very seriously that I should not go to Berlin. He knew, he said, that the stories of people disappearing were true, and had friends who were victims of Stalinist terror. I told René about our conversation, and we dismissed it with a laugh, thinking that he was the taken in by the propaganda of his friend Arthur Koestler.

I suppose it was partly René's charm that persuaded me to join him in his return to Germany. He was very good-looking and lively and it was fun to be with him. He was also extremely generous, not only with money, but in letting me lead my own life as an artist, which later included travelling separately. At first most of our expeditions were together, but when the children came, one of us had to stay at home. Sometimes it was I who had to suppress my envy of the marvellous trips to Japan and Cuba and other places provided by his function in the UNESCO artists' committee, but sometimes he had to manage without me too. Our family holidays on the Bulgarian Black Sea coast were a great pleasure, and our trip together to Geneva, to visit his family, was a very happy one.

I would have wished to accompany him more often, but I think sometimes he wanted to be on his own, and I understood that too.

A beach on the Usedom peninsula, at the German Baltic Sea.

17

History, Stephen said, is a nightmare from which I am trying to awake.

Ulysses, James Joyce, 1882–1941

In the early sixties, I received a letter from the Irish poet John Hewitt, then director of the art gallery in Coventry, saying that he had received the catalogue of a GDR exhibition, and was surprised to read that I had been born in Belfast. As he was once director of the Ulster Museum there, he thought he knew all the Belfast artists. He invited me to exhibit in Coventry, and I gladly accepted. The GDR Ministry of Culture, then campaigning for the recognition of GDR, took over the organization, even printing the catalogue with a text from Werner Klemke, which Hewitt would have preferred to write himself. He made a nice speech at the opening and had invited the famous Irish actor Michael MacLiammóir to attend, which greatly impressed my mother, who accompanied me to Coventry. We found that John Hewitt was an old friend of my headmaster in Belfast. They had been together in the left-wing movement there. Alec Foster was one of the founders of the Wolfe Tone Society in 1965, the aim being that Catholics and Protestants should be educated together in the cultural and political heritage of Wolfe Tone. It was the bicentenary of this founder of the United Irishmen, whose execution had been ordered by the British in 1798. The Wolfe Tone Society provided an impetus for the civil rights movement at the end of the sixties. I saw John Hewitt a few times again when my brother-in-law Hugh Clegg was appointed Professor of Industrial Relations at Warwick University and moved to Kenilworth, but then the Hewitts moved back to Belfast.

I had last been over there just after the war, when I went on a short trip with René so that he could meet my family. Granny had become a gentle little old lady, with a shawl round her shoulders and a footstool. She and René liked each other very much, which was strange as they came from such different backgrounds. There was little sign of war in Ireland. Food had always been plentiful, the Republic had been neutral, and there had only been just a few German air raids on Belfast, mostly near the docks. During one raid our house had been hit by firebombs and the upper floor burnt out. I had the impression then of being in a quiet backwater. When the situation escalated in August 1969, I was curious and wanted to go there, but as I could only travel on professional grounds, I went to the newspaper *Neues Deutschland* and asked if they would send me over as special correspondent, which they agreed to do. So I took on a journalist's job for which I had no experience, but it enabled me to get in close touch with the situation and the leading people in it. I stayed in a hotel in the middle of Belfast where most of the journalists stayed, and when there was a loud bang I rushed out to see what had happened, whereas the other journalists just changed elbows leaning on the bar.

At that time British soldiers had just been sent over to Northern Ireland to take over the duties of the police force, which was in bad repute because of its active antagonism to the Catholic section of the population and had been confined to barracks. The Catholics had won the sympathy of the public in England and were enjoying the ready ear of the press for their long-endured injustices. I contacted the civil rights movement and was able to see a side of Belfast I had never explored before, the Catholic Falls Road area, which had barricaded itself off, with burnt-out cars and rubble, because of the Protestant bully boys who marched around the Shankill with heavy sticks in their hands, looking for trouble. Between the Protestant Shankill Road and the Catholic Falls Road the army had put barriers of barbed wire. Bewildered British soldiers in battledress squatted beside machine guns on the corners. We went through an entrance guarded by a few men, sitting round a coke brazier, into the area which called itself 'Free Belfast'. In the little red-brick houses a news-sheet was being printed; folded and distributed by the children of the neighbourhood. The participation of the children in the battles of the street has caused some concern among onlookers, but as long as they are part of a threatened community, it is perhaps better for their psyche if they can take an active part. There was a touching cheerfulness, enthusiasm and optimism among these people at this time, which contrasted with the nervous, tense atmosphere we encountered in the Protestant part of Derry.

Derry is on the border of the Republic, and there the Catholics are in the majority. In the Catholic Bogside area we met Bernadette Devlin, looking very young, with long hair, knobbly knees in pale stockings and black patent shoes. 'Wee Bernadette' was then a sort of Joan of Arc to the Civil Rights Movement. In the red-brick rows of houses in Derry's Protestant district, with murals of William of Orange on the walls, white-faced women looked at us obvious strangers with hate and fear and pressed into our hands leaflets with pictures of policemen wounded by stones thrown by Bernadette and her supporters.

No one knew then how long all this would last. Ten years later, John Hewitt organized another exhibition of my work in the Arts Council Gallery in Belfast. I was put up in a hotel in the respectable university area. I was told that this hotel had been bombed by the Catholics, because they had accommodated a Protestant film team. Then it had been bombed again, this time by the Protestants because they had put up a Catholic film team. From the insurance they had been able to build a new wing. Not to worry because they were now paying protection money, and to both sides, and anyway hotels were not on the list at the moment, just prominent people. Three days after the opening of the exhibition a bomb went off near the City Hall and blew in the windows of the gallery.

When I was in Belfast in 1969, I went for a walk down York Street of course. I was surprised to see the Ulster Bank standing there intact, massive and frowning, familiar as an aged relative. The burnt-out section had been rebuilt, and it looked as it had always looked. It gave me quite a turn. I almost expected my father to emerge, complete with hat and stick, and walk down to the paper shop.

I wandered up Earl Street and saw that the little houses, built in the 1840s or so, were mostly deserted and falling apart. On a later visit I saw that the bank was empty too, with broken, dusty windows. The area was to be bulldozed to make way for a motorway to the docks, and the last time I was over, there was a space on the corner, planted with grass, and three young green trees where the old Ulster Bank had stood. The old tobacco factory looked shabby and naked, and there was a clear view over to the cranes of the docks. The dust of our house had joined the smoke that hangs over the city and drifts out over the estuary to the open sea.

With Irish poet John Hewitt at an Arts Council exhibition by Elizabeth Shaw in Belfast, 1979.

18

In the spring of 1944 Londoners developed an especially sharp sense of hearing. It was the time of the buzz bombs. As I have said already, the night they first arrived we went down to the street shelter and we saw that the sky was illuminated by anti-aircraft fire and what seemed to be a large number of small aeroplanes crashing down to earth. These were not in fact planes at all but rockets, Hitler's V-1 weapon with which he had sworn to put an end to the war. They were called buzz bombs because first of all one heard a 'buzz buzz', which grew increasingly loud. When the noise became exceedingly loud, it was advisable to take refuge under the nearest table. When the buzz suddenly stopped, there was a moment of silence, and then an explosion. If you heard the explosion, you could breathe again, you were alive. The V-1 weapon was followed by V-2, which did not have a preliminary buzz, just an explosion like a landmine. Both had no definite target, were meant to induce terror, and both came from the experimental rocket station of Herr Werner von Braun and others on the charming island of Usedom.

About thirty years later I visited Usedom for the first time.[1] I had rented a small room in Ückeritz, on the edge of a beech forest. I climbed up a hill and, looking over the treetops, I gazed down at a tranquil landscape, on one side the brackish Achterwasser, on the other the wide blue sea. It was a Caspar David Friedrich landscape. Apart from the light rustle of leaves and the gentle hum of insects there was no sound. A falcon circled overhead, deer moved silently among the trees, sometimes a hare passed on soft paws. I sat still in the silence, alone up there.

I was on holiday on my own for the first time ever. I could have sought a companion, but I wanted to have a real rest after my bereavement. I took along some books that I had long intended to read – a history of the Arabs, a little old history of Italy and a biography of Countess Markievicz, who had taken part in the Irish uprising of 1916. On the first day after my arrival, the weather turned grey and unfriendly. I woke up in the little room with an outsize wardrobe and a feeling of panic overwhelmed me. Why on earth had I come on a lonely holiday to this unknown place!

Repressing my urge to take the next train home, I went down to the beach, walked fifteen kilometres along the windy shore to the resort of Ahlbeck, ate in a smoky overcrowded restaurant, took the train back to Ückeritz and fell into bed, where I slept till the next morning. I set out in the rain in the opposite direction towards Wolgast, as if fleeing from myself. On the third day I spoke to myself sternly: 'This stay is not to be looked on as a holiday but as medicine to accumulate reserves of strength!' Just then the sun came out. I took my sketchbook and made some drawings from the top of the hill, took a bath in the cold sea, breathed the fine air of the forest and began to read my history books. On the fourth day I thought: 'Actually I don't need any company! I am quite happy alone with my various occupations.' Then I thought, 'If I go on like this, I shall become an egocentric eccentric!' And so I decided that on that very afternoon at three o' clock I would visit some artist colleagues, whose addresses had been given to me. I called round uninvited, woke one from an afternoon snooze, disturbed the other at work, but they were hospitable and nice. My loneliness was forgotten. I continued with my fresh air, sleep and bathing therapy, but I had found new friends and knew where to go when I was tired of myself. I lay in the sun on the beach, a swan rocking on the quiet sea, or I sat on a moss bank in the green woodland and read my histories of wars – won, lost, forgotten. I thought about victories, and defeats, about the little victories over one's self, about the big victories such as the Arabic invention of the numeral '0', about the defeat of countless hordes of greedy warriors. I thought about this place, where not so long ago Nazis in brown uniforms were strutting about – hard to believe for one who had not experienced it – and of how Bertolt Brecht had written '*Der Schoß ist fruchtbar noch, aus dem das kroch,*' meaning it could happen again, that eruption of brutality and aggression from which no country is immune, it seems.

19

Here and there. Abroad. At home. I travel very often, and I like it, being curious. From time to time, I have had occasion to visit Leipzig, not to visit the famous fair, but to attend the jury of the competition for the best-designed book of the year. The trains leave rather early, and I usually fall asleep, but I try to be awake when we go through Wittenberg so that I can look back at one of my favourite views: the old towers of Wittenberg, seen across the wide, calm River Elbe. Twice I have left the train at this station to spend a few hours looking at the town. Hamlet went to school in Wittenberg, at a time when the place was in turmoil. I was there by chance in 1968, at the time of the student revolts in Europe, and as I examined the documents about student unrest in the sixteenth-century university, I noted the similarity to present events. During the Reformation, Wittenberg University was a centre of new ideas, a refuge for critical opinion and new ventures. William Tyndale from England, fleeing persecution because he tried to translate the Bible into English, came to Wittenberg to visit Luther, who had succeeded in translating it into German. It was here too that Luther pinned his famous thesis to the door of the church and so proclaimed the Reformation. Wittenberg University no longer exists. At the time of Napoleon, it was attached to the University of Halle. Luther's house still exists, and is preserved as a museum, as well as the house of Philipp Melanchthon, Professor of Greek at the former university and an influential personality during this renaissance of thought. There is another little museum in Wittenberg that has little to do with Luther's sober ideas. It is a collection of African and Oceanic art, fantastic masks and other requisites of witchcraft. All that and the paintings of Cranach make a visit to Wittenberg well worthwhile, but the train goes on, passed the stinking chimneys of Bitterfeld, pouring out yellow smoke that spreads over the countryside, and finally reaches Leipzig.

The *Encyclopaedia Britannica* of 1911 describes Leipzig as the city that contains the largest university in Germany, the seat of the Supreme Court of Justice and the most influential centre of music and literature in Europe. At this time Leipzig had not quite achieved its zenith, however, for the station, which was planned to be largest in the world, was only completed in 1915.

Here we are, in it. Grey and enormous, with high arches to absorb the steam from the trains, a huge cathedral of the railway age. Since the time of the salt trade between Halle and St Petersburg this has been a crossroads for many countries in Europe who took part in the Leipzig trade fair. If one goes down one of the many staircases and out of one of the many exits one is in the middle of Leipzig, and there are the Leipzig trams, noisily operating in both directions with great speed and a ringing of bell – a great danger to those non-Leipzigers who attempt to cross over without using the pedestrian underpass. The number of drunks who hang around the station, as well as the children who dart out without warning, must yield a rich harvest of victims. The tram drivers need strong brakes and have them, as one of our jury members found out when he was flung against the door and had to be led bleeding to a first-aid station.

Leipzig is not only an international trade centre but a centre of book production. Severe censorship in the other great book centre of Germany, Frankfurt-am-Main, at the end of the seventeenth century, induced many printers to move to Leipzig.

The international jury for the best-designed book took place in the solid building of the German Library. The jury sits from morning to evening at a long table, and a pile of books is passed from one to the other: the quality of the binding, the cover, the typography and the illustrations are examined. A plus or minus, with the initials of the jury members, is then jotted on the paper and laid inside the book. For me this was a lesson in the art of making books. At first, I tried to conceal my ignorance about typography and other technical matters, but I listened to the judgement of the professors and began to develop an opinion of my own. A steady flow of coffee and rolls, thickly spread with butter, *Wurst* and cheese prevented us from fainting.

In Leipzig I got to know a different kind of artist. Formerly I had moved among wild painters, sculptors and excitable journalists and at first I did not know what to make of these book people. Their behaviour was calm, and when we talked together and did not discuss books they spoke of chrysanthemums and canaries and not of politics and world-shaking events.

Elizabeth Shaw, Wieland Herzfelde and Werner Klemke at the award ceremony for the Käthe Kollwitz Prize, 1981.

The first book artist that I encountered was Werner Klemke. Our paths crossed shortly after the war in the *Ulenspiegel* editorial office. I observed his passion for book design and typography. He asked me to visit the famous typographer of the *Times*, Stanley Morison, on my next trip to London, to deliver greetings and a book from Klemke. There in the *Times* office I met another neat, well-dressed book man, who received me politely and accepted the message.

In the fifties Karl Gossow, art director of the Aufbau publishing house, asked me to illustrate the fables of Gellert, an eighteenth-century writer. Horst Erich Wolter, who presided over the Leipzig book jury at that time, asked me to be a member. Professor Wolter was rather plump, gentle and modest, and when he lovingly held up a book for discussion, he reminded me of a quotation from Walt Whitman: 'Camerado, this is no book, who touches this touches a man.'

But no – it was not our affair to concern ourselves with the text. We should keep our distance and judge the form, not the content. The well-known book designer Albert Kapr was a leading figure in the book field then. I first met him in a Leipzig theatre during some event. We were introduced, and he stared at me blankly. As we approached the wardrobe, he took my coat, but continued to stare. 'Really?' he said, 'Are you really Elizabeth Shaw?' I was rather embarrassed as he followed me closely into the theatre. 'But you look so normal!' he said.

I liked the company of the book people, in the jury, as well as in the hotel, during our evening gatherings, but I only obtained a fleeting impression of Leipzig itself. Near the German Library there is a Russian church, built as a memorial to the 22,000 Russians who fell in the battle of Leipzig against Napoleon. Its golden tower is a landmark in this part of Leipzig. One day I looked in after a jury session and found a Greek Orthodox service taking place. It was reminiscent of an opera, doors before the altar opened and closed, as the priests appeared to bless the congregation, surrounded by icons donated by various Russian churches. The congregation consisted of three young men who sang the litany in Russian. They remained standing during the entire service, and as there was no instrumental accompaniment it was probably similar to all church services during the Middle Ages.

Once I went to the Leipzig Museum of Fine Arts, which is to be found in a massive building that was once the High Court of Justice of the German State, and where the famous trial of Dimitroff by the Nazi Göring took place. There is an interesting collection of painting and sculpture, including a number of works by Max Klinger, who lived from 1857 till 1920, and whose work was unknown to me. Like Rosetti and his school in England, he was out of fashion for a long time, but as the abstract movement shows signs of fatigue and is losing its public, the strange morbid visionary painting and sculpture of Klinger has become interesting again. His foreboding sculpture of Cassandra suggests the calm before a storm. I seemed to detect his influence on the work of Käthe Kollwitz, as well as the Norwegian Munch. His sculpture of Beethoven now stands in the concert hall, the Leipzig Neues Gewandhaus. In the centre of Leipzig there are quite a few foreigners to be seen, not only because of the fair, but because it is a university town. Students wander over the old marketplace past the ancient town hall, where I was proud and happy to receive the Gutenberg Prize of the city, a distinction reserved for book people. Not only for this reason I am fond of Leipzig. In this sombre city the great Baltic scholar Kuno Meyer lived for a time and died. He published a great deal of Irish poetry, founded the School of lrish Learning in Dublin in 1903, and in 1911 he was professor of Celtic in the university of Berlin. His translations of Irish lyric into English are the best I know. One of them introduces this book.

20

O but we dreamed to mend
Whatever mischief seemed
To afflict mankind, but now
That winds of winter blow
Learn that we were crack-pated when we dreamed.

from 'Nineteen Hundred and Nineteen', W.B. Yeats

At the end of the summer of 1971, when the disturbances in Northern Ireland had reached a sullen stalemate, I went over for a short holiday. The steamer from Liverpool entered Belfast in a heavy sea fog. It glided cautiously through the thick whiteness. A ship's officer stood rigidly in front, sounding a bell when a buoy was passed. Otherwise only the faint swish of water and muffled moan of foghorns were audible in the hushed air. The passengers, mostly Irish labourers on their way home from work in England, sat huddled in their coats, apathetic and sleepy after a rough night crossing. A few British soldiers in battledress leaned silent and gloomy on the rails. As we docked, we met the unsmiling stare of tense commandos on the quay. I walked to the station through empty streets except for a few grim-faced dockers on their way to work. Not a city that invited one to linger and I was glad to be on my way out of this oppressive air to another Ireland, for a brief stay in the west of the Republic, in the little village of Rosses Point on the Atlantic coast. Arriving in Sligo in the late afternoon, I found a small hotel near the old harbour where swans circled in the swirling water of the incoming tide. 'Will you be staying long?' asked the frowsy landlady, shooing away a tinker with a baby on her arm who was begging at the door. 'Only just tonight,' I said, 'I'm going on to Rosses Point tomorrow.' So she didn't bother to change the sheets, as I discovered later – not that I cared much, after sitting up through a stormy night on the ship.

Rosses Point, County Sligo.

I spent that evening in the town hall nearby, where the Sligo Drama Circle were playing Synge's *The Shadow of the Glen*. Early next morning I took the bus a few miles out along the estuary to Rosses Point. I had no trouble in finding a room in the village. It is not far south of the border between the Republic and Northern Ireland and a large number of holidaymakers come from Derry, even from Belfast. 'There haven't been many this year,' said my landlady, 'sure they'd be afraid to leave their homes. They'd be burnt down if they left them empty.' Rosses Point is a fishing village on the tip of an estuary, surrounded by wide sandy shores. On one side rises Ben Bulben, on the other side the long line of the Ox Mountains, stretching out to the wild, stony landscape of Connemara. The swift flowing waters of the bay reach into Sligo, and in the middle of the current stands an iron figure, painted red and blue, in a sailor's costume of the early nineteenth century, known as the Metal Man. He holds a lamp to guide the fishing boats through the sandbanks to the open sea.

The poet W.B. Yeats came from near here and the tourist industry has named it 'Yeats Country'. 'Wasn't Yeats a Protestant? I didn't think he'd be so popular down here,' I remarked meanly to a nice man who gave me a lift one day. 'No Irishman is ever any good till he's dead!' he replied. The following morning, I set off with sketchbook and umbrella to walk cross-country to Drumcliffe churchyard where Yeats is buried. The inlet of Sligo Bay runs along the side of the whitewashed houses of Rosses Point village street, the water moving fast. Here Uncle Pat threw my father in to teach him to swim and put him off that sport for life. Here beneath the lush fuchsia hedges with their exotic red and purple flowers is Memory Harbour, curiously named, and painted by Jack Yeats, brother of the poet. 'Like all artists who achieve a degree of universality, Yeats is closely bound with the local and particular,' wrote John Berger in *The Life and Death of an Artist*. 'Cezanne seems formalised until one has seen Provence through his eyes. Yeats seems too mobile, over spontaneous, until one has watched the west coast of Ireland. And watched is the word, for the landscape there is a fast series of events, not a view – an unchanging structure. The land is as passive as a bog can be. The sky is all action.'

Drumcliff Bay and Ben Bulben, County Sligo.

At the end of the village I turned up northwards up a lane that ended in a quarry. I followed a track through long wet grass to the right and decided to take my shoes off before they were wet through. It was pleasant to walk barefoot, the clean wet mud squelching between my toes, and the best way to go in this moist land of no snakes. I crossed a style into a field on top of the rise. Grey, lichen-covered rocks showed through the grass in which grew pale blue harebells and the rare pure white flowers called grass of Parnassus. Brown and white butterflies fluttered in the sun over clumps of yellow whin and purple heather. Then I was startled to hear rifle shots not far away. 'To be shot for a partridge in this country of dead heroes would be a silly end,' I thought, hastening down the hill. In the shallow valley I washed some of the mud off my feet in a small clear pool, edged by green rushes, and then climbed to the top of the next hill. From here there was a magnificent view over Drumcliffe Bay. The blue rippling water lay between me and green Ben Bulben Mountain. A flock of clouds rested on its heights and beneath I could see the grey spire of Drumcliffe church. I sat down on a sun-warmed rock to draw the landscape.

There was no one in sight, only a small black cow, which turned its head and looked for a while with inquisitive anxiety, then went on grazing. A gust of soft rain landed on my drawing and I decided to move on. As far as I could survey the route from above, it seemed that it would be necessary to walk round the bay by the road and would take longer than I had reckoned. I put on my shoes when I reached the road and walked along looking for a turning to the left, where I could cut across to Drumcliffe.

Suddenly I was startled by a voice behind the hedge. 'It's a fine day!' said the voice, and then – slightly aggrieved because I did not answer at once – 'How are you, now?' I had forgotten the courteous friendliness of country people, but I was better prepared when I inquired the way further on. An old man told me that it was possible to cut across the bay when the tide was out, but he would not advise it. I should go on to the main road, then turn left. 'Isn't it a lovely day!' he concluded, and I agreed. It was raining heavily just then but I knew what he meant: he wished it was a lovely day because it would be pleasant for us both if it was.

Illustration from *The Little Black Sheep*, 1985.

In spite of his advice I turned into a steep lane leading down to the bay, where I met a lady coming up towards me. She greeted me gaily, as if we had just met at a party. 'To Drumcliffe!' she exclaimed. It was possible to go that way: 'But you'd be lost in the shucks with your white shoes! You can get a lift on the road.' She accompanied me to the main road. 'I'd come with you myself to Drumcliffe, but I have to hurry now!' Along the main highway, I saw a tourist horse-drawn caravan, as advertised, 'Tour Ireland at leisure!' The caravan was like a large open tin can, painted and turned on its side. A gloomy young man with a beard sat in front, holding the reins, another walked behind. On the roadside opposite some tinkers were camping, clothes spread out on the hedges. They had turned in the horse-drawn vehicle and travelled with a fine motor-trailer. A milk van stopped and offered me a lift so I drove down to the church, a stopping point for tourist coaches. Beside Yeats' grave there is the ruin of an ancient Irish round tower to be seen, and a thirteen-foot-high sculptured stone cross, both dating from Celtic Ireland before the twelfth century, during that great period of Irish art that also produced those ornate and curiously oriental-looking illuminated manuscripts. The grave of Yeats lies near the entrance to the church.

'Under Ben Bulben's head,
In Drumcliffe churchyard Yeats is laid.'

I walked around, looking at the graves of the small landowners and farmers of the Cromwellian plantation, my ancestors, who have largely died out in the district. A year before, driving through here with a brother, we called at the house of my grandmother's family, a lonely farm on the edge of the brown Ox Mountains, and found a cousin still living there. Unexpectedly we were received with some coolness and reserve at first, unusual in these parts. When we had clearly identified our relationship, Cousin Pat explained that the week before some Americans had called at a neighbouring farm, claimed that it was their ancestral home, drank them dry and then went on to the next farm with the same story. Cousin Pat rose and produced a bottle labelled 'Rose's Lime Juice' from the corner of the kitchen cupboard, hesitated suddenly and asked: 'Are you Pioneers?' 'No!' said my brother hastily. He had been a student at Trinity College in Dublin and knew what was meant. The Pioneers were members of the temperance movement launched in the nineteenth century by Father Mathew, whose statue stands in the middle of Dublin's main street, together with other national heroes, including the man who founded the waterworks. So we all had a drop of poteen, that powerful brew which is illegally distilled in the countryside. Now the ice was melted, the curly-haired wife produced photographs of the children, all of whom had left the country and were working in England.

My grandmother's family, the McKims, were of Celtic stock, and there is a rumour, which I like to think is true, that some of our ancestors were the O'Clerys, who wrote a famous history of Ireland called the *Annals of the Four Masters* in the sixteenth century. I hope that this is true. It atones for these Cromwellian grandfathers. It is said that the O'Clerys changed their name to Clarke to avoid persecution and adopted the Protestant faith as it was then advisable to do. Cousin Pat had returned to the Church of Rome however, by marrying a Catholic. Their prosperity had not increased. The house had an even more impoverished look than when I had seen it last, many years ago. The front was shut up and entrance was through the back.

Indeed many must have been turning in their graves in Drumcliffe churchyard, for the barrier between the Protestant and Catholic sections had been removed and the graveyard is claimed as a national memorial by a Republic dedicated to Catholicism. I sat on the ivied wall and did a sketch of the ancient cross. As I sat there, regular coachloads of sightseers were unloaded. They examined Yeats' grave, stretched their legs and were off in a cloud of fumes. It began to rain lightly again, and I set off on my return journey. I thought I might try a shortcut across the estuary from this side. I slithered down a bank by the bridge and took my shoes off again. I went along a green cattle track and over a rushy field to the edge of Drumcliffe Bay. The rain had stopped. The strong Atlantic tide had receded, leaving about two miles of hard, brown, ribbed sand with little rivulets trickling in between, glittering in the afternoon sun as they pursued the outgoing tide.

I began to walk across to the opposite bank. It was much further than I had expected, and remembering how rapidly the tide had receded, I realized that it could advance equally fast and remembered too that the old man had advised against a short cut. I began to hasten until I was within reach of the other side. However, I need not have panicked because the wide expanse of sand still stretched out naked and wet to the far rim of the waves with no one in sight except a black speck of a man gathering shellfish among a patch of seaweed. The banks of the estuary were hollowed out by the waves and, between the yellow whin bushes on top and the line of seaweed below, grew little sweet-perfumed clumps of purple daisies with plump juicy stems. Towards the shore rose high sand dunes covered with long spiked grass. On the other side of the strand, Lissadell House, once home of the Countess Markievicz, was visible through the trees. She acquired this un-Irish name as an art student in Paris where she married a Polish count. Later she took part in the Irish national movement, and at the age of forty-eight, in a green military uniform, she commanded a contingent of Connolly's Citizen Army during the Easter uprising of 1916. She was sentenced to death, later reprieved and in 1918 elected first woman member of the British Parliament. In 1919, however, she became

Minister of Labour in the insurgent Irish republican government instead. She opposed the Irish treaty of 1921 which divided the country into two and remained a militant republican member of the IRA until her death in 1927.

The sun shone on Lissadell Strand, the sea was blue and there was no one in sight, so I stripped and had a bathe in the clear water, drying myself with a handkerchief. Then I walked over the rocks to the next beach. The rocks were thickly crusted with pinkish coral and molluscs and in between were small clear pools where red sea anemones waved their tentacles and drifts of tiny shells lay on the occasional patch of sand. On the beach of Rosses Point a few holidaymakers were strolling and two young men were exercising their caravan horse on the edge of the waves. At sunset the light on the mountains changed yet again. I climbed up past the caravan site and the Yeats Country hotel to the village and my room over the pub. A glass of Guinness and a large cheese sandwich. What more could one want.

Exactly a year later I was sitting in a restaurant near the harbour in Baltshik on the Bulgarian coast. It was midday and extremely hot. The air smelt of dust and stew. We had fled from the white stony hills to the nearest shade and were eating oily aubergines with a glass of white wine. Two bewildered little old pink-and-white ladies joined us at the table and asked our assistance in ordering something to eat. Their soft accents told me that they were from Dublin. They said that they were doing a five-day tour of Bulgaria, an audacious undertaking that was part of the new tourist agreement between Bulgaria and the Irish Republic. I mentioned that I had visited Rosses Point the year before. 'Ah! I go there every Easter!' said one of them. We smiled at each other and I remembered with serenity the wide, ribbed, empty sands with little waves lapping at the edge, the mild air and soft rushes of rain, the small, rare flowers and the clouds moving among the mountains – the extraordinary tranquillity that exists beside the strident unrest in this country of contradictions.

Jonathan Swift.

21

'When Adam delved and Eve span, who was then the gentleman?'

Quotation from John Ball's sermon

There is no equality in the western world, and if socialism ever claimed it, it was during the tyranny of uniform Maoist China. At a time of material shortages, inequality begins. In eastern Germany, after the war, the system of ration cards was graded: workers in heavy industry, academics and various functionaries received the highest rations, reasonable enough. Housewives and pensioners received the lowest. Housing distribution gave priority to those anti-Nazis who came out of prison or emigration. The Soviet Union had a list of people to whom they awarded food parcels according to their importance. There was the 'Big Payok' and the 'Small Payok', similar to the American 'Care' parcels, and both disappeared about the same time.

The system of privileges – such as being a patient in a government hospital, having access to special holiday homes, living in certain quarters – arose later and was guarded and secret. It is actually based on a kind of barter. When bricks are scarce and you have tiles, you can come to an arrangement. I remember once being with my son in a builder's yard, when he leapt hastily into his car to follow a lady on a bicycle through devious paths because he had heard her say that she wanted to sell old drainpipes. 'But you don't need drainpipes!' said I. 'But I know someone who does, and he'll give me wooden planks for them!' replied my son.

Illustration from Karl Marx. *Englischer Alltag* [Everyday Life in England], 1968.

Illustration from Karl Marx. *Englischer Alltag.*

Illustration from Karl Marx. *Englischer Alltag.*

If you have power in the form of a function, you can distribute boons in exchange for services. One of the most sought-after privileges for the young is to be on the 'Travel permitted' list, and this may entail certain sorts of obsequious behaviour. Fortunately travel for private reasons is becoming easier in recent times.

There is one category of people who have the privilege of going abroad for up to three months of the year if they wished and from whom no return was demanded, and that is the old-age pensioners. They can buy rail tickets to West Germany and back for GDR currency and there was a time when I could do the same for England. In 1981 I went to the railway office and asked for a return. The lady behind the counter looked at my passport to see if I had an exit permit and said: 'You are a pensioner?' 'Yes,' said I, wondering. 'Then you can only buy a single ticket to London, not a return.' 'And how am I supposed to pay the fare back?' I asked, for one is not permitted to possess any money abroad. 'Owing to the generosity of our government, you receive a good pension here. If you can bring a letter from the mayor of the town where your relatives live in England, stating that they are too poor to pay your fare back, you can buy it here.' Was she pressing me to stay or go for good? Owing to my loud widespread complaints, a kind friend who often travels to London came to my rescue. 'I'll buy your return ticket for you,' he said, and so he did. It was illegal, of course. My London visit came to an end, and then there was the chore of packing, sorting out, squeezing things in. Now when one leaves the GDR as a resident, one fills out a yellow card, which was then torn in half, and on return the second half was presented. For purposes of statistics, they say. 'I can't find my damn yellow card!' I said to my nephew, who was driving me to Liverpool Street Station. 'Well, be humble!' he advised wisely. I had decided to take the day ferry from Harwich to the Hook, and the night train from the Hook to Berlin for a change. The harbour was full of young people with enormous packs on their backs and we swung through the ticket control at a great rate.

Elizabeth Shaw, 1980.

Only that evening in the train, did I realize what had happened. The Dutch guard who came to punch my ticket looked at it carefully and said, 'But this is a ticket from London to Harwich only!' Then I realized that in the scramble at the frontier the wrong piece had been torn off. 'You must buy a new one!' 'I have no money! I can give you a GDR cheque?' 'I must go and inquire.' Later two guards came in. 'You can see from the sum on the outside flap that I paid both ways,' said I. 'The train goes through to Poland. We will ask the engine driver if he will take a GDR cheque.' After a time three guards came back and sat down. 'We are awarding you a free trip through Holland. You must see what happens when you reach the West German border.' It seemed that not many travelled with the night train. I was alone in the compartment, which was a good thing, because it is easier to deal with officials without witnesses. When the West German guard came, I said, '*Mir ist ein kleines Malheur passiert* – I have had a little mishap! The wrong half of my ticket was torn off at Harwich, but the Dutch inspector said it was alright because the price on the cover indicates that I paid the return fare!' The ticket man respected his Dutch colleagues. 'That's all right then,' he said. Now I had only the GDR border to worry about, and I thought that would be simple enough. I could even offer a cheque. It was about two in the morning, so I stretched out on the seat to have a little sleep. We reached Hanover, where the train waits for a long time. After a while I heard the carriage door open softly, and pretended to be asleep, hoping for no company. Then I opened one eye and saw a scruffy looking young man standing beside me, one hand in my handbag, which was open and ready to produce passport and ticket at the next frontier. I don't know which of us was the most startled. He made for the door, stammering some kind of apology. I debated whether to raise an alarm, but in the dark and silent station I was too afraid. No more sleep for me anyway. The GDR ticket puncher came. '*Mir ist ein kleines Malheur passiert!* But the Dutch and the West German colleagues said it was alright!' He could not but agree. In Friedrichstraße Station, Berlin, at last, I proceeded gaily to passport control. '*Mir ist ein kleines Malheur passiert!* I have lost my yellow card!' '*Ein kleines Malheur?* This is a serious matter!' said the passport man sternly. 'Go and sit on that bench, I will inform my superior.' A superior officer appeared, took my passport, and went into a back room, to look up my dossier, no doubt. After a time, he returned and gave me a new yellow card. I went through passport control and landed at customs. The same senior officer was there and examined my bag purposefully. 'What are you looking for?' I asked. 'Your yellow card,' he replied, and as if he had some kind of instinct, he searched and rejected until he plunged a hand into a plastic bag and drew out – indeed, my old yellow card. 'Well!' he said, 'You are causing a lot of trouble so early in the morning! Now we have two yellow cards!' 'Tear one up!' I suggested, but it seemed this was too simple a solution, and I left him with his brow bent, grappling with some incomprehensible statistical problem.

22

The wall that divided Berlin provided a background for spy thrillers which has not been rivalled since Conan Doyle invented the hansom cabs rattling through Baker Street and the London fog. Just as many believed that Sherlock Holmes really existed, so many were convinced that Smiley, the secret agent of *The Spy Who Came in from the Cold,* and the background of the stories were quite real. The books of Le Carré and Len Deighton and others greatly conditioned public opinion in the western world as regards the socialist countries.

When we first came to this city, we thought of it as a focal point in post-war development. We considered ourselves internationalist with a cosmopolitan outlook and belonged to that happy company of artists and writers who find common ground wherever they were born and wherever they may happen to meet. Much later, when I lived alone, I began to integrate more closely into my immediate environment. I had to speak German more often because my grandchildren did not speak English. I did not only speak more German, but I began to read more in that language and to know more about German history. I slowly realized how little René and I knew about this country. In René's day we usually spoke English to each other because German was a foreign language for us both, and we had met in England, and anyway we thought it was a good idea to give the children the chance of growing up with two languages. However, when I addressed them in English, they answered very often in German. Only when we visited England in 1954 did they seem to realize that speaking English was not just a peculiarity of their parents. Our daughter listened carefully for a while; then she began with an entire sentence: 'There are a lot of snails in this garden!' she remarked in a high-pitched voice, which she did not abandon until we left for Berlin, when she returned to her usual guttural tones.

'*Zwei Berliner Kinder reisen nach England* [Two Children from Berlin Travelling to England]'. Cartoon drawn by Elizabeth of her children in England.

Although I did not know much about Berlin, on the way to the bank in what was then called Dorotheenstraße, I noticed a ruined church, which was surrounded by eighteenth-century gravestones with inscriptions finely engraved in French. A little research revealed to me the history of the Huguenots in Berlin and I began to bore my family with my constant reference to them; how the French Huguenots were brought to Berlin by the Elector of Brandenburg in the seventeenth century, how they had founded the Academy of Science, the Charité hospital, and introduced various French words like 'Portemonnaie' into the language. I think that my own partly Huguenot ancestry made Berlin seem a friendlier place. The ruins of that church and the old gravestones have long since disappeared, and the area is now a parking lot. There is, however, a reconstructed Huguenot church in the Platz der Akademie with a museum in the basement. One day, when walking along the Schönhauser Allee, I came across the Jewish cemetery in the neighbourhood of Senefelder Platz. I had heard of this cemetery when someone told me that the painter Max Liebermann, who was expelled from the Academy of Arts by the Nazis, had been buried there. Inside there was a vast green tangle of trees and overgrown bushes. As I walked among the gravestones, I realized what an enormous contribution the Jews had made to Berlin. The names of well-known publishers, bankers and big stores recurred frequently. Not only here, but in the still larger cemetery in the suburb of Weißensee – the largest in Europe I believe – there was evidence of the immense size of the Jewish population in the past. They had emigrated here in great numbers to escape persecution in central and eastern Europe. I did not find Liebermann's grave at first, so numerous were the paths, but I met a young man who led me to it and told me a little about the place. He explained that as the Jews were originally a nomadic desert people, they had the custom of placing pebbles on the graves they visited instead of flowers, and this custom was still observed. Occasionally I saw gravestones commemorating Jews who had died in the Nazi concentration camps, during those years of terror.

In 1981 I stood a ladder rather carelessly against the wall of my bathroom intending to give it a coat of paint, climbed up, the ladder slipped, I fell and broke my leg, which somehow got twisted between the steps. As I lay in hospital, my friend Alan Winnington came past and said: 'I have found a garden for you, but you must decide immediately if you want it or not!' So I bought my garden without having seen it, and for several years it was a great pleasure as well as a new experience for me, until I realized that the work involved was more than I could manage, and I handed it over to some good friends. Before that, however, I wrote a piece about it for the weekly *Weltbühne*, once the magazine of the Berliner writer Tucholsky. The title was 'My Garden':

> I have a garden. For the first time in my life. There is a patch of woodland in front, grass and flowerbeds at the back. There are two apple trees and one pear tree, which bears twelve fine pears every year. This is only because it is pampered and watered by me for months beforehand. Perhaps you might say that I could save a great deal of time and effort if I were to buy a couple of pounds of pears in the fruit shop, but then I can only say that you are not a gardener. I have a plum tree too, in fact several because new ones keep shooting up out of the earth. If I don't do something about this, I shall soon be living in a plum forest. There are two black, red and white woodpeckers living in my garden; a number of small singing birds; surprisingly, a lonely frog; and several slow worms. These last live in the compost heap, and since I noticed them, I don't like to turn it over, as they are a protected species. Under the soil live numerous ants, and when the sun shines, they come out of the dark secret world of roots and go about their busy business. I have bees too. They have settled in a crevice just over the door of the old wooden hut which stands in the middle of the garden. During the summer I was able to observe the life of the wild bees, whirring with their wings at the entrance to their nest, to transmit the news, that there is good honey to be found in my lavender blooms. We lived peaceably together until one day, as I was giving the door a coat of paint, I raised my arm in the direction of their nest. Immediately a sentinel bee swooped down and stung me in the face. Since

then, we respect the status quo of our territory. Apart from the bees there are various kinds of spiders and quite fantastic beetles. The bees hum, the birds twitter, and at the weekend rock music emanates from the neighbours. In the spring, as I bend over my rockery, I sometimes hear the loud call of the cranes, announcing their arrival. Then I drop everything and hasten through the forest, down to the damp green meadow to see the big grey visitors from Africa. They land briefly on the way up to Mecklenburg and stalk up and down, throwing back their heads and uttering their loud trumpeting cry, which is echoed in the forest. But back to the garden. Because I never had a garden before, I look tenderly and with amazement at the tiny wild pansies, the poppies and other plants which grow all over the place by themselves. My policy is laissez-faire, anything that wants to grow can grow, but then I notice that some plants seem to be getting the upper hand. Voltaire's Candide says 'It is necessary to tend our garden,' and this is just what I too have in mind, but I soon realize that gardeners must have a plan, they must be ruthless, and they must take a good look at the sort of territory they are managing. My garden has a sand and gravel soil. Whatever grows well in the south of France grows well here – lavender and thyme at least. Desert plants should thrive too, I thought, but my lilies remain stunted and rarely bloom. Maybe the bulbs are being nibbled by voles? But I have seen no trace of these little creatures for some time. They may themselves have been eaten by the slowworms. The ancient law of the jungle rules.

The woodland part of my garden in front looks rather like a jungle. But I'll get to work on that soon. I am so busy with planting and digging and marvelling that I have no time to organize grills and garden parties. My neighbours must find this strange, but I think they have got used to me by now. For me, this autumn 1986 is an anniversary. Forty years have passed since sculptor and painter René Graetz and I came to Berlin in that tumultuous time between the end of the war and the beginning of a new era. Forty years of happy picture-making – my work and pleasure. I have written the occasional text as well, but my German, I regret to say, is still faulty. Nevertheless, I have become a Berliner. I have a garden.

Illustration from *Gittis Tomatenpflanze.*

23

Life is like playing a violin solo in public and learning the instrument as one goes on.

Samuel Butler, *Selected Essays*, 1855–1902

I live in Treskowstraße in the north of Berlin. This suburb with its high houses was built about 1900. Most of the stucco decorations are chipped and broken, a few have been renewed. It is not so long ago since the last statue of Bismarck was hauled down from a gable in Kurt-Fischer-Platz, formerly Bismarck Platz. The fire brigade had to fetch a longer ladder to reach him, and the old ladies stood about watching and muttering to each other: 'They haven't managed to get the Iron Chancellor down yet!'

There is a sycamore tree in front of the house in which I live, which is probably as old as the house itself, and from my window on the second floor I can look right into its green foliage and live on a level with the birds chirping in its branches. It compensates a little for the stink of petrol rising from the increasing traffic down below. This part of the city was developed during the peak of German expansionism shortly before the First World War. On the pavement in front of the house I live in is the name of the drug-store owner who built it in the days of Kaiser Wilhelm, picked out in black and white mosaic. 'Max Noa' still looms large on the street before the shop window, though Herr Noa himself has long since gone, and the name of the present owner is illuminated over the front door. Other enterprises are emerging – a private baker, an upholsterer, a central-heating repair firm, fill gaps not covered by socialist industry. As time passes, the house fronts are being renovated one by one, the chipped decorations removed, bullet holes plastered over.

At the end of the Treskowstraße a large supermarket has taken the customers of some smaller shops. There are good parking facilities outside, and outsiders as well as locals buy there on their way out to the country at weekends, causing queues to lengthen. On Saturday mornings in the summer a brass band plays in front of the store, conducted by a plump old Berliner.

Opposite me live a youngish couple, who were at school with my son in-law. When they aren't washing clothes, they are washing windows and, in the morning, they wash themselves and then lean out of the window, half-naked. If I happen to be doing the same, our glances meet, and we hastily withdraw. Below them used to live an old lady who spoke with a Bavarian accent and was very friendly. She often stood outside on her small balcony, surveying the street and greeting passers-by. One day, and on succeeding days she was not there, and I supposed she was dead. Then I noticed, beyond the lace curtains, a shadowy figure waving at me. At first, I thought it was a ghost, but she emerged again on the balcony and I was so happy that I bought a bunch of flowers and rushed up to present them to her. She said that she had had a cold. Now she really is dead and her daughter lives in the flat with her husband. Not long ago she called on me unexpectedly with some roses – evidently my impulse had gone on record. I didn't ask her in because I was in the middle of something. Now she avoids me when we pass on the street. I don't know why. Maybe I broke some rule of etiquette. There are so many I have never quite mastered, like the use of '*Du*' and '*Sie*' in addressing a person. René told me, 'All artists call each other *Du!*' but when I did, the artists looked startled, as if I was making improper advances. As for shaking hands, even if in doubt, it is better to do it. Little children on their way to school shake hands with each other, like politicians, indicating favour or disfavour. Almost opposite me lives the parson of the Lutheran church down the road. He does not wear his collar backwards as in England, in fact he wears a shirt and jeans and does not look like a parson at all. He has a noticeboard at his gate, which advertises not only church services but various ecological causes as well. His ten-year-old daughter, who likes my children's books, visits me occasionally and we play Halma or pick-a-stick or something like that.

She is very well behaved and does not only wipe her shoes on the doormat but offers to take them off as well. Looking out of my back window, I can survey the state of private enterprise, which has a steadier relationship with the authorities than the church. In the yard there is a small firm that repairs refrigerators for restaurants. It used to be run by the father, now the son has taken over. They have a villa in the suburbs with a swimming pool, are very industrious, and have extended their workshop sheds in all directions. They are quiet, polite and, as far as I can see, unpolitical.

At the corner of the street is the post office, and there, as well as in the supermarket, one meets friends and neighbours, and we stop for a chat. Maybe this sounds like a village anywhere, but chats on the street are often interrupted by the loud roar of a plane landing. I can see them from my balcony, swooping down beyond the houses. They are landing in Tegel airport in West Berlin, just across the Wall, a reminder that this is a very special village, the divided Berlin. Now the frontier is crumbling, the line of confrontation between East and West. 'Never,' said a fifty-year-old man once to me, 'have I known life without fear: fear of the Nazi teacher at school, who used to walk through the classroom, hitting those who made a mistake on the back of the head; fear of bombs during the war, fear of the enemy, fear of defeat, then fear of a new war, of the atom bomb, not to speak of the widespread net of state security.'

As I write, something astonishing, moving, is happening. A new generation has grown up. Their grandparents were crushed by the Nazis; their parents grew up during the Cold War; but the youngest generation is learning to express itself. They have already learned that governments can be overthrown. They demonstrate courage, and the age-old strength of solidarity. I am glad that I came to Berlin. But maybe the question is not so much why I came to Berlin as why I stayed?

I remember a day in 1948, shortly before I left on a trip to England. I went along the street in Zehlendorf, looking at the small German paving stones and sensing the foreign, disquieting atmosphere, and I remember thinking, 'I won't come back! I'll stay in England!' But after a peaceful rest, I thought again, and recalled the absolute commitment of a group of people in Berlin, of whom I had become a part, and missed them.

'Sometimes,' I once said to my brother-in-law much later, 'I wish that I had married a nice tweedy Englishman and lived in the lovely English countryside!' 'You wouldn't have liked it, Lizzy,' he replied, 'You would have had to drive your tweedy children to school every day – no, it would have been nothing for you'

So instead I witnessed the rise and fall of the GDR. When times change, one looks upwards. I take a walk to the end of the Treskowstraße, past the supermarket into the Waldstraße where the sky is wider and look to see if Ozenfant's stars are still there.

There they are, blinking away in the great unknown.

AFTERWORD

MEMORIES OF A UNIQUE LIFE JOURNEY IN ART AND LITERATURE

Elizabeth Shaw's memoir is a unique and substantial contribution to autobiographical writing and to Irish migrant literature. The text brings us on a life journey that traverses Ireland, Britain and the former German Democratic Republic (GDR). It engages with Irish nationalism, Ulster Protestantism, internationalist communism, radical art, newspaper caricatures, children's writing, the cities of Belfast, London and (East) Berlin, the German Baltic Sea and the Irish Atlantic coast; especially Sligo and Drumcliffe churchyard, where most of the extended Shaw family, we are told, lie buried. It is the story of an artist who believed in the political impact of her work, while it also addresses questions of identity and geographical location that are as pertinent now as they were in Shaw's time.

Shaw's memoir was originally written in English – the text preceding this afterword is not a translation but the original version. The author lived and worked for over half of her life in East Germany – and became a key figure in that country's literary and visual art landscape – but still felt more at home in her first language. Shaw completed the text in the late 1980s, shortly before the fall of the Berlin Wall; an event which had a domino effect and culminated in the collapse of the Soviet Union and its extended empire. The memoir was translated into German by Wolfgang de Bruyn, and the German-language version was first published in 1990 for a German-speaking audience under the title *Irish Berlin: Wie ich nach Berlin kam* [Irish Berlin: How I Came to Berlin], followed by a second edition in 2013. However, the original English-language version – Elizabeth Shaw's narrative in her own words – has until now never been published. This is the first edition that makes Shaw's life story accessible to a wider English-speaking readership and also introduces readers to her work as a book illustrator and caricaturist – work which has remained largely unknown in the anglophone context.

A memoir is a narrative of self and often what is not said, what is left out of the process of turning a subjective view of one's own life into text, can tell us as much perhaps as the actual text itself. Elizabeth Shaw does not tell the reader very much about her level of success in the GDR, and indeed outside of the GDR, as a children's writer and illustrator. The reason for this could simply be that the text itself was written with an East German reader in mind, a reader who would have been aware of her work and may have been curious about Shaw's origins. This may also be suggestive of Shaw's humility, her desire not to be at the centre of things and to avoid too much attention. Her unpretentious personality is something frequently commented on by her friends and family members in interviews.

Elizabeth Shaw was one of the most successful children's book illustrators and authors of the GDR, while she also made a name for herself through her book illustrations and caricatures for adult audiences. Born in Belfast in 1920, Shaw had decided to become an artist at the age of four and was further encouraged by her art teacher at secondary school in Bedford, in the south of England, where the family moved when Shaw was a teenager. She went on to study at the Chelsea School of Art in London, enjoying the city's cultural life and exciting arts scene, as she details in her memoir. Here she attended classes by Hugh Finney, Graham

Sutherland and Henry Moore, and was influenced by French avant-garde painter Amédée Ozenfant, while increasingly focusing on book illustration and caricature. Henry Moore praised her illustrations for Emily Brontë's *Wuthering Heights*, which she had entered for a scholarship competition, and which already showed a style that was to become characteristic for her work.

When Shaw describes her growing interest in internationalist, left-wing ideas during her time in London, this reflects both a general mood and dominant discourses among younger artists and intellectuals in the city. London was home to a large exile community in the 1930s and 1940s, with most of its members advocating internationalist ideas. The cosmopolitan student culture Shaw found herself in drew on these ideas, but also on British and Irish working-class culture and its political discourses. Through friendships with fellow students at the Chelsea School of Art, Shaw became increasingly involved with communist groups and attended pacifist political meetings. Sean O'Casey's play *The Star Turns Red*, which was first staged by the London Unity Theatre in 1940, struck a chord with many left-wing students in the face of fascism's spread across Europe. With the outbreak of the Spanish Civil War in 1936, many students felt they had to take a clear stance. Shaw remembers how she discovered communism as a political movement 'that strove for an international order without war or social injustice [...]',[1] which made her turn away from her earlier romantic idealization of Irish nationalism. For the student of fine art in London reading the *Communist Manifesto* (1848), Marxism seemed to offer a solution to the social inequality she had witnessed in Belfast as a child. This is how the author remembers her introduction to communist ideas when looking back on her life in the 1980s.

Shaw began to publish sketches in 1940; she designed political posters, contributed to the London left-wing magazines *Our Time* and *Lilliput* and exhibited works in 1943 at the Artists' International Association in London. In 1942 she met the Berlin-born, Geneva-raised artist and anti-fascist René Graetz. They married in 1944 and, similar to other German exiles opposed to National Socialism, they idealistically felt that by moving to Berlin in

1946 and contributing to the newly emerging German cultural landscape as artists they could help build a 'better' Germany.

Shaw commenced publishing caricatures of everyday life in post-war Berlin, including one of a self-important policeman chasing children away from a tiny lawn between ruined buildings, with a sign saying: 'To walk on the grass is *VERBOTEN!!*' (1946). When the *Ulenspiegel*, a left-wing satirical journal she contributed to, had its licence withdrawn in 1950, Shaw began working full-time for the principal GDR national daily newspaper *Neues Deutschland*, which faithfully reproduced the party line. Her drawings of that time, reflecting contemporaneous GDR foreign policy positions, thus tended to be anti-western, meaning largely and explicitly anti-militarist and anti-US.[2] However, Shaw stopped working as a caricaturist for *Neues Deutschland* in 1953, after Rudolf Herrnstadt lost his position as the paper's editor-in-chief. Having expressed his understanding for those GDR citizens who took part in the workers' protests in East Berlin on 17 June 1953, Herrnstadt was removed both from the SED's Central Committee and his position in *Neues Deutschland*. In spite of setbacks, Shaw gradually established herself as a quality name in East German caricature. In 1959 she received a major commission from the East German Academy of Arts to draw portraits of all forty-three Academy members, including internationally well-known figures such as the author Anna Seghers, the actress and director Helene Weigel and the composers Paul Dessau and Hanns Eisler. Other works included illustrations to Bertolt Brecht's texts in *Ein Kinderbuch* [A Children's Book] (1965).

Shaw's skilfully simple, ironic style, influenced by French and English caricature, brought something new to the East German cultural landscape of the time. In *Sozialistische deutsche Karikatur 1848–1978*, published by the East Berlin Eulenspiegel Verlag, she is mentioned as one of the most important young caricaturists and illustrators of the GDR: 'The artist combined in her style ironic sharpness or a delicate sense of humour with a distinctive grace. This style was suitable both for the optimistic, humorous visual interpretation of our own successes and the bitter, satirical reckoning with imperialism.'[3] While her husband René Graetz's work was branded as 'formalist' and therefore marginalized in the early 1950s, when the East German art scene was dominated by Stalinist cultural politics prescribing a Socialist Realism, which left little space for greater artistic freedom, this does not seem to have affected Shaw's own work. Despite having developed her own distinct and individual style, Shaw's drawings did not radically challenge the official discourse, neither aesthetically nor content-wise.[4]

Applying this comic-like style for children's book illustrations marked Shaw, however, as unconventional. Elizabeth Shaw was forty-three years old when she turned to writing children's books herself. When she presented her first two stories, *Der kleine Angsthase* [The Timid Rabbit], and *Gittis Tomatenpflanze* [Gitti's Tomato Plant] to the biggest publishing house for children's literature in the GDR, the Kinderbuchverlag Berlin, in 1963 she initially met some reluctance. Cartoon-like illustrations in children's books were new at the time, in both parts of Germany. But the books were an instant success, and the Kinderbuchverlag asked Shaw for more books. Until 1990 she published fourteen further picture books, almost all with the Kinderbuchverlag – including *Zilli, Billi und Willi*, a re-telling of the story of the three little pigs, and *Bella Belchaud und ihre Papageien* [Bella Belchaud and her Parrots] about an eccentric elderly lady who owns birds that recite Shakespeare. Both books were awarded the prize for '*Schönstes Buch*' [the most beautiful book] by the German Booksellers' Association of the GDR, an award Shaw received ten times in total. A further two of her books were published in 1996 and 2000 – following her death and the end of the GDR – and six anthologies of her illustrated children's stories were published between 1983 and 2008. Shaw writes that she had initially become interested in children's books because she found illustrations too conventional and decorative in style in the books then available. She had already begun to illustrate children's books, as well as books for adult readers by other authors, in 1951. Thus, she illustrated works by Bertolt Brecht, James Krüss, Nikolai Nossow, Hans Fallada, Rainer Kirsch and Astrid Lindgren. Among the many books for adult readers illustrated by Shaw are Karl Marx's *Englischer Alltag* [English Everyday Life] (1968), for which she also won an award, and works by Mark Twain.

Shaw herself compared her motivation to write children's books that communicated a moral message in a comical manner and appealing to children, with the same 'missionary spirit' she applied to her humorously-intended political caricatures:

> I wrote mostly very moral tales, trying to put across certain values such as courage, kindness and living for something bigger than oneself, because I have this missionary spirit that prompted me to do political cartoons. Anyway, children are very moral too and have a strong sense of justice until it is dispersed by the adult world. Some of my stories are just fun, because adults are often so solemn and children like fun. Once I saw an old Italian grandpa sitting in a clothes store in Berlin and translating one of my books for his grandchild, both laughing heartily. That pleased me greatly.[5]

Readers could laugh about and at the same time identify with characters such as the Timid Rabbit, slightly stocky and with large fearful eyes, who is an outsider, marginalized by the village community because of his fearful nature, until he overcomes this and helps someone who is smaller and weaker than him. At the same time, her success also provided financial stability to a household with two artists as income-providers. Because of her limited German, Shaw continued to depend on support when writing her texts in German. She sometimes asked her own children for help when encountering language problems in the process of writing.

Der kleine Angsthase [The Timid Rabbit] became the most popular children's picture book in East Germany and has apparently not lost its appeal for young readers. It has seen twenty reprints, the most recent in 2024, and has regularly been staged. Elizabeth Shaw's books are fondly remembered by many who grew up in East Germany, and who now buy her books for their own children and grandchildren. The *Angsthase* can be found in bookshops, but also alongside Spreewald gherkins in tourist shops and on websites selling products from the former GDR, having become something of a cultural icon.[6] Shaw's books have been translated into several languages, and have found a readership across Europe, albeit less so in western Europe. However, both author and work have remained virtually unknown in Ireland. *The Timid Rabbit* was first published in English by the British publisher Sadler & Brown in 1967, and by O'Brien Press in Dublin in 2007. Other books by Shaw which were translated into English in the 1960s for the British market include *Tortoise Has a Birthday* and *Sammy Wins a Cup*. The only book by Shaw first published in Ireland before being translated into German was *The Little Black Sheep*, published by O'Brien Press, Dublin in 1985, and translated into various languages, including Irish.

To some extent, it is the perspective of an outsider that gives Shaw's caricatures and picture books their particular quality. They are humorously informed by a sense of distance to the people and situations she encountered in her everyday life and in the circles of '*Kulturschaffende*'; cultural creators as they were called in the Communist Party language, in East Berlin. Like the *Angsthase*, being something of an outsider was a recurring experience for much of Shaw's life – from her childhood in Belfast and the school years in Bedford to the time as an Irish, or Irish-British, person in Berlin. While she herself perceived her identity as predominantly Irish, during her time in Berlin England appears to have been as much of a home for her as the north of Ireland. What emerges from her autobiography is a hybrid identity – located somewhere between Ireland, Britain and Berlin, between her Irish familial roots, her family in England and her artist community in London and Berlin. In 1954 Elizabeth Shaw took her children with her to see friends and family in Devon, Essex, Oxford and London for an extended holiday. English was the main language in the Graetz/Shaw household. Shaw's daughter, Anne Schneider, remembers her mother telling her and her brother Irish stories and singing English nursery rhymes and songs.[7] These found their way into a collection of rhymes, translated by Margaret Hellendall and Heinz Kahlau and illustrated by Shaw, published under the title *Ping Pang Poch* (1967). In a passage on Leipzig in her autobiography, Shaw recalls that she fell in love with the city due to its links to Kuno

Meyer, a late nineteenth-century and early twentieth-century German Gaelic scholar who had studied in Leipzig, who later became a professor in Berlin and was highly influential in relation to the study of the Irish language at universities in Ireland.

Shaw also visited Northern Ireland in 1969 and wrote two articles for *Neues Deutschland* about the emerging 'Troubles', which are deeply sympathetic to working-class Catholic communities. Here she depicted the British state in Northern Ireland in colonial terms and suggested that the coming together of both the Catholic and the Protestant working classes, as well as republicanism and socialism, represented the only possible solution – an argumentation in line with an emerging left-wing republican position and with the tradition of Belfast communism, which looked beyond sectarian divides, as represented by such working-class Protestant figures as Betty Sinclair.[8] Having visited Belfast and Derry in 1969, she returned to Belfast in 1979 for an exhibition, curated by the poet John Hewitt. She was also able to spend short holidays on the Irish west coast, travelling to her ancestral home area in Sligo in 1971, and visited Glengariff and Youghal on different occasions. Her work on the Irish edition of *The Little Black Sheep* led to another visit to Ireland in the 1980s.

From her memoir it is not quite clear if Shaw was completely aware of her own privileged position as a member of the cultural elite of the GDR, but she writes about friends who suffered political oppression. The Shaw writing in the mid-1980s is critical of the naivety of the young and somewhat unquestioning Shaw of the 1950s. The narrative voice of the text is also aware that her frequent travelling to places outside of the GDR and other socialist states is a distinct privilege as a British passport-holder. She would like to have this privilege bestowed on everyone in the GDR. She expresses support for the emerging protest movement in the East German state in the 1980s, while remaining a supporter of socialism and of socialist countries. As Elizabeth Shaw and her husband, René Graetz, were both foreigners who frequently travelled abroad and who had wide and varied contacts beyond socialist countries, the Ministry for State Security, the infamous Stasi, kept a close eye on both of them. As Shaw and Graetz were public figures, their files are open and available to inspect in the Stasi archives. There are files from the mid-1960s and the early 1970s that deal with both Shaw and Graetz. A 1966 report, containing a number of factual errors, details contact with England and West Germany, as well as listing the couple's extensive travels abroad, but concludes that both figures are essentially politically 'dependable'.[9] A report from 1970 suggests that René Graetz was becoming more critical in relation to GDR art and society and reflects on conditions for a possible observation of both. An observation does not however appear to have taken place, or at least there is no record of this.[10]

Thus, although Shaw and Graetz were essentially members of the GDR cultural elite, they also remained simultaneously suspicious in the eyes of the GDR state due to their position as outsiders who held a number of foreign contacts. They lived therefore in and became a part of the GDR state but existed at the same time outside of it, as 'others' and outsiders. This is also what makes Elizabeth Shaw's narrative voice so unique – her position both inside and outside of East Berlin, Belfast and London.

Shaw left behind an extensive collection of drawings and illustrated books. In 2023 Elizabeth Shaw's daughter, Anne Schneider, handed over part of her mother's artistic estate to the Staatsbibliothek zu Berlin [The State Library of Berlin]. Over 1000 original illustrations, 150 sketches and several sketchbooks, both for her published works and unpublished material, are now held in the state library's Children's and Youth Literature Department, offering further insights into her work. In 2024 the original drawings of the illustrated books for adults were given to the Deutsche Buch- und Schriftmuseum [German Museum of Books and Writing] at the German National Library in Leipzig.[11]

Shaw's *How I Came to Berlin* evokes a Berlin and its people at a very specific historical time and under a specific political system, in many ways distant from the contemporary, highly globalized and consumerist German metropolis. In other ways, it is actually a very contemporary everyday story of globalization – a migrant's story, the life story of someone finding herself both as an outsider and insider – but most of all this is a narrative of cultural merging and the creation of something new. The 'newness' that is created and reflected upon here is unique, drawn from Ireland, Britain and the GDR but contemporary migrants will also surely see aspects of their own story echoed in Shaw's text.

Sabine Egger & Fergal Lenehan

2025

SELECTED WORKS BY ELIZABETH SHAW

The following is partly based on the list included at the end of Shaw's *Wie ich nach Berlin kam* (2013) and ordered chronologically. When no place of publication is mentioned in an individual entry, the title was published by Der Kinderbuchverlag Berlin in East Berlin. Only translations of books by Shaw into English are mentioned for additional information, not translations into other languages.[1]

Children's books written and illustrated by Elizabeth Shaw

Der kleine Angsthase. 1963 (*The Timid Rabbit*. Trans. R. Sadler. Chalfon St Giles: 1967; Dublin 2007).

Gittis Tomatenpflanze. 1964.

Die Schildkröte hat Geburtstag. 1965 (*Tortoise has a Birthday*. Trans. R. Sadler. Chalfont St Giles, 1967).

Wie Putzi einen Pokal gewann. 1967 (*Sammy Wins a Cup*. Trans. R. Sadler. Chalfont St Giles 1968; Toronto 1968).

Bella Belchaud und ihre Papageien. 1970.

Bettina bummelt. 1971.

Zilli, Billi und Willi. 1972.
Das Bärenhaus. 1973.
Als Robert verschwand. 1975.
Guten Appetit. 1976.
Die Schöne und das Ungeheuer. 1982.
Der scheue Schneck. 1984.
The Little Black Sheep. Dublin 1985 (*Das kleine schwarze Schaf*. Trans. E. Shaw. 1989).
Die fleißige Familie. 1986.
Wildschwein Walter. 1988.
David und die Kühe. 1990.
Das einsame Zicklein. Munich 1996.
Die Landmaus und die Stadtmaus. 2000.

Collections

Das kleine Shaw-Buch. 1983.
Lustige Elizabeth-Shaw-Geschichten. 1987.
Miezekatz und Huckelpuckel. Leipzig 1997.
Das dicke Elizabeth-Shaw-Buch für die ganze Familie, ed. by P. Graetz. Berlin 1999.
Geschichten für Kinder. Weinheim 2007.
Mehr Geschichten für Kinder. Weinheim 2008.

Autobiographical texts and collections of drawings

Eine Feder am Meeresstrand. Berlin (East) 1973.
Spiegelbilder. Berlin (East) 1983.
Irish Berlin. Trans. W. de Bruyn. Berlin, Weimar 1990.
Wie ich nach Berlin kam. Eine Irin in der geteilten Stadt. Extended Edition. Berlin 2013.

Children's books illustrated by Elizabeth Shaw

Wolf, F., *Tiergeschichten.* Berlin (East) 1951.
Krüss, J., *Spatzenlügen und andere seltsame Begebenheiten.* 1957.
Anderson, E., *Hunde, Kinder und Raketen.* 1958.
Berger, K.H., *Eine fröhliche Reise,* 1959.
Mara, V., *Das Mädchen MAX und 10x Fax.* Berlin (East) 1959.
Anderson, E., *Großer und kleiner Felix,* 1961.
Nossow, N., *Freundchen und andere heitere Geschichten,* 1963.
Wilke, U.J., *Helle im Tor,* 1963.
Berger, K.H., *Das Kutschpferd und der Ackergaul,* 1964.
Brehm, E., *Die erfrischende Trompete.* Berlin (East) 1964.
Brecht, B., *Ein Kinderbuch.* Berlin (East) 1965.
Kästner, E., *Das Schwein beim Friseur,* 1965.
Hellendall, M.M. (ed.), *Ping, pang, poch. Englische Kindergedichte.* Adaptation Kahlau, H., Trans. M.M. Hellendall and E. Shaw, 1967.
Holtz-Baumert, G., *Von lustigen Wichten, zwölf kleine Geschichten,* 1968.
Dehmel, P., *Von morgens bis abends,* 1969.
Fallada, H., *Der getreue Igel,* 1970.
Lindgren, A., *Lillebror und Karlssohn vom Dach,* 1971.
Kahlau, H., *Schaumköpfe,* 1972.
Dickens, M., *Das Haus am Ende der Welt,* 1975.
Kirsch, R., *Es war einmal ein Hahn,* 1975.
Sostschenko, M., *Tintenfässer aus Brot,* 1977.
Medek, T., Siewert-Medek, D., *Kindergarten-Liederbuch.* Frankfurt/M. 1979.
Spies, L., *Mein Liederbilderbuch,* 1982.
Rennert, J., *Wie der Elefant entstand,* 1982.

Other books illustrated by Elizabeth Shaw

Ausschuss f. dt. Einheit (ed.), *Dein Gewicht entscheidet,* Berlin (East) 1954.
Twain, M., *Kapitän Stormfields Besuch im Himmel,* Berlin (East) 1954.
Fürchtegott Gellert, C., *Fabeln,* Berlin (East) 1956.

Grodzienska, S., *Der Gänsemarsch*, Berlin (East) 1956.

Wiens, P., *Zunftgenossen, Kunstgefährten*, Berlin (East) 1956.

Brecht, B, *Gedichte und Geschichten*, Berlin (East) 1958.

Twain, M., *Humoristische Erzählungen*, Berlin (East) 1958.

Max Schroeder zum Gedenken, Berlin (East) 1959.

Konstantinow, A., *Der Rosenölhändler*, Berlin (East) 1959.

Stein, H.J., *Reportage aus dem deutschen Jenseits*, Berlin (East) 1961.

Stein, H.J., *Wallfahrt nach Walpurgisland*, Berlin (East) 1961.

Brehm, E., *Die erfrischende Trompete / Taten und Untaten der Satire*, Berlin (East) 1964.

Kusche, L., *Quer durch England in anderthalb Stunden*, Berlin (East) 1964.

D. Day, *Skizzen eines Globetrotters*, Berlin (East) 1965.

Jerome, J.K., *Drei Mann in einem Boot*, Berlin (East) 1967.

W.K., *Der Mann, der Karate konnte*, Berlin (East) 1968.

Marx, K., *Englischer Alltag*, Berlin (East) 1968.

Kunze, H., *Bibliophilie im Sozialismus*, Berlin (East) 1969.

Kusche, L., *Wie man einen Haushalt aushält*, Berlin (East) 1969.

Kusche, L., *Patientenfibel*, Berlin (East) 1971.

Waterstradt, B., *Alle Tage ist kein Alltag*, Berlin (East) 1974.

Kusche, L., *Vorsicht an der Bahnsteigkante*, Berlin (East) 1975.

Kusche, L., *Die fliegenden Elefanten*, Berlin (East) 1977.

Bodeit, B. (ed.), *Seit ich dich liebe. Gedichte von Frauen aus zwei Jahrhunderten*, Leipzig 1977.

Kusche, L., *Knoten im Taschentuch*, Berlin (East) 1980.

Ichenhäuser, E., *Erziehung zu gutem Benehmen*, Berlin (East) 1983.

Kusche, L., *Leute im Hinterkopf*, Berlin (East) 1983.

Twain, M., *Werkausgabe*, 1984.

Kusche, L., *Der Mann auf dem Kleiderschrank*, Berlin (East) 1985.

Kusche, L., *Nasen, die man nie vergisst*, Berlin (East) 1987.

Kusche, L., *Der Opa hat ein Schwein verschluckt*, Berlin (East) 1989.

ENDNOTES

PART I

CHAPTER 2

1 Goraghwood Railway Station in County Armagh was opened in 1854 and closed in 1965.

CHAPTER 3

1 Belcoo, County Fermanagh.

CHAPTER 5

1 All art works by Elizabeth Shaw, except where stated.

CHAPTER 6

1 Éamon de Valera was President of the Executive Council of the Irish Free State from 1932 to 1937. He was Taoiseach of Ireland/Éire from 1937–48, 1951–4 and 1957–9. He was then President of Ireland from 1959–73.

2 The Austrian-born Max Reinhardt (1873–1943) was one of the formative directors of modern theatre.

CHAPTER 7

1 This comment probably derives more from the anonymous street ballad "The Wearin O' the Green", which refers to the aftermath of the 1798 rebellion, rather than any actual legislation or factual events.

2 Charles Stewart Parnell was leader of the Home Rule movement, which sought a parliament in Dublin and internal autonomy for Ireland within the British Empire.

3 Theobald Wolfe Tone was sentenced to death, but died before his execution.

PART II
CHAPTER 1

1 This is a reference to Thomas Bewick (1753–1828), a printmaker and illustrator important for reviving the art of wood engraving and establishing it as a major printmaking technique. See: https://www.britannica.com/biography/Thomas-Bewick.

CHAPTER 2

1 Shaw actually attended the Chelsea School of Art. The 'Chelsea Art School', which was a different entity, closed in 1907. See https://www.artbiogs.co.uk/2/schools/chelsea-school-art. Where the name 'Chelsea Art School' is incorrectly used by the author, it is replaced by the correct name 'Chelsea School of Art'.

2 C.E.M. Joad (1891–1953), a British philosopher author and radio personality of the time, who was also agnostic and a pacifist. See: https://www.britannica.com/biography/C-E-M-Joad.

CHAPTER 3

1 Elizabeth Shaw may mean here a double saut.

CHAPTER 6

1 *Der Sturm* (transl. The Storm) was a German avant-garde art and literary magazine founded by Herwarth Walden, covering Expressionism, Cubism, Dada and Surrealism, among other artistic movements. It was published between 1910 and 1932 and impacted on international art trends during its time.

CHAPTER 7

1 This is likely a reference to the Sri Lankan-born Tamil poet Meary James Thurairajah Tambimuttu (1915–1983).

2 This likely refers to Indian-born Tamil writer Ka. Naa. Subramanyam (1912–1988).

CHAPTER 9

1 According to the author's daughter, Anne Schneider, Gustav Emil Graetz had already moved to Switzerland by 1902.

2 This is a reference to Russian-born Herbert Vladimir Meyerowitz (1900–1945) and his German-born wife Eva (1899–1994), whose maiden name was Lewin-Richter. See: https://www.britishmuseum.org/collection/term/BIOG134107.

CHAPTER 10

1 The American-British sculptor Jacob Epstein (1880–1959).

PART III
CHAPTER 1

1 According to the author's daughter, Anne Schneider, this refers to Gerry and Miriam Wolff.

2 Karl Schmidt-Rottluff (1884–1974). His Expressionist paintings were viewed as 'degenerate' by the Nazis and he was given a '*Berufsverbot*' (an occupational ban). His paintings were later also viewed sceptically in the GDR, where the socialist realist style was favoured.

CHAPTER 2

1 White Russian here may either denote someone from Russia who opposed the Bolshevik Revolution or may be read as the earlier term for Belarussian, which was also White Russian.

2 The architect Bruno Taut (1880–1938). See: https://bauhauskooperation.com/wissen/das-bauhaus/koepfe/biografien/biografie-detail/person-Taut-Bruno-1470.

CHAPTER 5

1 The caricature refers to Germany being split up into French, British and American zones (and does not feature the Soviet Union).

CHAPTER 6

1 Hermann Bruse (1904–1953), Arno Mohr (1910-2001) and Horst Strempel (1904–1975).

2 Ernst Thälmann (1886–1944), was a well-known communist and politician in the Weimar Republic. He was imprisoned by the Nazis and murdered in Buchenwald concentration camp, near the city of Weimar, in 1944. In the GDR Thälmann was eulogized as a hero and a role model.

CHAPTER 7

1 The Paris Agreements ended the occupation of West Germany and created a sovereign state. In line with GDR propaganda, this is represented by Shaw as West Germany implicitly remilitarising.

2 This refers to David Low (1891–1963), a New Zealand caricaturist who worked in the UK for, among other publications, the *Evening Standard* and the *Guardian*, and the German-British Victor Weisz (1913–1966), who drew under the name 'Vicky'. As a Jew and a socialist, Weisz left Germany in the 1930s and worked in Britain for, among other publications, the *Daily Mirror* and the *Evening Standard*.

3 This was the collective name given to the work of the Soviet caricaturists Mikhail Kupriyanov (1903–1991), Porfiry Krylov (1902–1990) and Nikolay Sokolov (1903–2000).

CHAPTER 8

1 Selman Selmanagić actually died in 1986 in Berlin.
2 The inscription on the drawing refers to Brecht's short story "Herrn K's Favourite Animal".

CHAPTER 11

1 A Sorbian minority also exists in the Oberlausitz area of eastern Saxony.
2 This is the English translation of *Der Mann in der Schlangenhaut*, the German name given to Sidney Lumet's 1960 film *The Fugitive Kind*, starring Marlon Brando. The film was based on a play by Tennessee Williams.

CHAPTER 16

1 Henri Kay Henrion (1914–1990), was a Nuremburg-born graphic designer who had a successful career in Britain from 1936.

CHAPTER 18

1 Shaw's husband, René Graetz, died in 1974.

AFTERWORD

1 See this volume, pp. 149.
2 See F. Lenehan, 'Elizabeth Shaw from a Transnational Perspective: The Intercultural Self, Propaganda and Shaw's Representation in the GDR Print Media'. In: D. Byrnes, G. Holfter and J. Connacher (eds), *Perceptions and Perspectives: Exploring Connections between Ireland and the GDR*, Trier 2019, pp. 103–22.
3 K. Haese, 1945–1978, V. In: H. Olbrich et al (eds), *Sozialistische deutsche Karikatur 1848–1978. Von den Anfängen bis zur Gegenwart*. Berlin 1983, pp. 276–372; here pp. 278.
4 See S. Egger, 'Elizabeth Shaw (1920–1992): The Irish Caricaturist who Left Her Mark on East German Children's Literature.' In: S. Egger (Ed.), *Cultural/Literary Translators: Irish-German Biographies II* (Irish-German Studies 9), Trier 2015, pp. 71–94, pp. 82.
5 See this volume, pp. 58.
6 See S. Egger, 'The unknown Irish writer behind an East German children's classic.', *RTE Brainstorm*, 8 July 2021. https://www.rte.ie/brainstorm/2021/0706/1233384-elizabeth-shaw-der-kleine-angsthase-the-timid-rabbit/.
7 See Egger, 2015, pp. 86.
8 See Lenehan, 2019.
9 F. Lenehan, 'Belfast Woman Elizabeth Shaw's Stasi File'. *History Ireland*, November/Dezember 2024, pp. 36–8.

10 See Lenehan, 2024.

11 Other works by Elizabeth Shaw and René Graetz are held in the Kunstarchiv Graetz und Shaw. See kunstarchiv-graetz-shaw.de.

SELECTED WORKS BY ELIZABETH SHAW

1 This list, with references to English translations. was first published in Egger, 2015, pp 90–93.

INDEX